THE
UNITED
STATES
of PIZZA

THE
UNITED
STATES
of PIZZA

CRAIG PRIEBE
with DIANNE JACOB

Photographs by Jeff Kauck

AMERICA'S
FAVORITE PIZZAS,
from THIN CRUST *to*
DEEP DISH, SOURDOUGH
to GLUTEN-FREE

RIZZOLI
NEW YORK

New York · Paris · London · Milan

Acknowledgments

We are deeply indebted to Steve Crown for his generosity in making this book possible.
Thanks to our agent, Carole Bidnick, for a second opportunity to write about pizza.
Editor Christopher Steighner made astute improvements to both our manuscript and book design.
Photographer Jeff Kauck contributed spectacular, creative photos. Toni Tajima designed our clean and
stylish look throughout. Our meticulous copy editor Tricia Levi kept us on track.

I am grateful for my wonderful wife, Wendy, who eats pizza tirelessly with me, cleans up after my messes,
and makes each day of my life special with her beautiful smile and a keen sense of culinary adventure.

—CRAIG

Thanks to my husband, Owen, for enthusiasm and clean-up skills. Kris Diede was a godsend in the kitchen.
Colleagues Rosemary Mark, Mary Margaret Pack, Greg Patent, and Jennie Schacht provided culinary expertise.

—DIANNE

First published in the United States of America in 2015
by Rizzoli International Publications, Inc.
300 Park Avenue South
New York, NY 10010
www.rizzoliusa.com

© 2015 Craig Priebe

2015 2016 2017 2018 / 10 9 8 7 6 5 4 3 2 1
Distributed in the U.S. trade by
Random House, New York
Printed in China

ISBN-13: 9-780-7893-2944-8
Library of Congress Control Number: 2015934254

To Steve Crown &
the Crown family

Table of Contents

Introduction

One of the most fascinating things about American pizza is how it changes depending on location. In New York and Brooklyn, pizza is thin crusted and bendy, with cooked tomato sauce and a layer of cheese. In Chicago, pizzerias make thick, pielike pizzas loaded with cheese and meats. In California, crispy wood-fired pies showcase seasonal vegetables, while in Louisiana, a Cajun pie might feature spicy crawfish.

I love them all, from the old-school pizzas at family-owned restaurants to the hipster minimalist pies at new pizza joints. *The United States of Pizza* celebrates all kinds of pizzas including the regional and lesser known, from coast to coast. These include Grandma and Grandpa Sicilian pizzas in the Northeast, a red-sauce-striped pan pizza in Detroit, and a St. Louis-style pizza with a baking powder crust.

I didn't know about all the varieties of pizza until I started researching this book. While the country is currently obsessed with thin, wood-fired crusts topped with a dab of sauce and a bit of mozzarella, there is more—so much more—to enjoy. There are meat-stuffed strombolis to dip into spicy tomato sauce, deep-dish cornmeal pizzas to cut into, and sourdough pizzas with puffy rims to chew. There are a few high-end pizzas made with duck proscuitto and lobster. Even gluten-free pizzas have taken hold, and in the last chapter, I've created a crispy crust that you will love, whether you're gluten-free or not.

Grilled pizza was a trend in 2008 when I published my first pizza cookbook, *Grilled Pizzas & Piadinas*, with my coauthor, Dianne Jacob. For me, grilled pizza was much more than a fad. I owned an award-winning grilled pizza restaurant in Atlanta for more than seven years. I also made pizzas for international competitions and won lots of awards, including an award for best overall pizza one year.

The recipes in *The United States of Pizza* are inspired by pies at all kinds of pizzerias, from the famous to the local, whether in Colorado, Brooklyn, or Hawaii. They are my interpretation of the restaurant's dish, created for you to try at home. (And if you want to try them at the restaurants, that's great too. Menus change, however, so check with the restaurant first to be sure the pizza is offered.) I've included a guide to all the featured pizzerias on page 186.

For each recipe, you'll find the name of the restaurant and its location, plus a little information about the place and the pizza. They say pizza is mostly about the crust, so I've organized the book by type of dough. You can bake your way through everything from New York–style to Sicilian-style pan pizza to whole wheat, corn flour, gluten-free, and more, depending on your mood.

This isn't a compilation of the Best Pizza in America—such lists are subjective and can change the moment a new place opens—but a snapshot of America's panorama of pizzas, from coast to coast. When I look at this book, I see the American ingenuity and the entrepreneurial spirit that firmly wedged pizza into our daily lives. I see the growth of new ideas and a vision of what gives our families reason to gather and break bread. I see our differences across the country and across the table.

But mostly I see our similarities, our common bonds that bring us to bake our pizzas and serve them to the people we love. It is America's favorite food.

It is easy to get into a complicated discussion about making pizza, like how long to proof the dough, which conditions are best for fermentation, or choosing the right acidity content of tomatoes. But that isn't necessary. I wrote the recipes as simply as possible, incorporating lots of the techniques and tricks I've learned over many years of research and cooking as a chef. My goal was to give you great flavor and textures without sacrificing authenticity and character.

For the last ten years, I have been the executive chef for Henry Crown & Company in Chicago, serving such dignitaries as President Barack Obama, former vice president Al Gore, and Nobel Peace Prize–winner Elie Wiesel. I have even served them pizza! That's because I have been obsessed with perfecting pizza for twenty-five years, and there's no end in sight.

Chapter 1

TOOLS and TECHNIQUE

I never tire of learning just one more thing that will make my pizzas magical. And then once I've mastered that thing, I keep hunting for another technique. Transforming flour and water into a crispy, crackling dough seems simple enough, but it has taken years of practice and experimenting to make pizzas good enough to win awards.

So before you flip through to the recipes, this chapter tells you about the tools and techniques chefs use that will help you make your pizzas rise from the delicious to the transcendent. The first section is all about the right tools for the job. Here are the mixers, pans, and other equipment I use most, plus a few thoughts on other items that make it easier to make a great pie. The second section walks you through pizza-making techniques, so you can get a feel for the process and learn some tricks of the trade. I also explain why dough needs an overnight rise, and how to shape it, how to add toppings for maximum effectiveness and taste, and how to work ahead.

TOOLS

Stand Mixer: I use this type of mixer for all my doughs, so you will need one too. Pizza dough needs a long kneading time, and a stand mixer makes the job easy and efficient. (If you want to mix dough by hand, see instructions in the techniques section.) I like KitchenAid stand mixers because they are powerful and get the job done quickly. One with an 8-quart capacity is best. Anything less is too small to mix pizza dough. Hamilton Beach makes good stand mixers too.

High-End Stand Mixer: This is totally optional, but if you're a dough fanatic, I recommend the Electrolux Assistant Bread Mixer. My model is the Verona Magic Mill DLX mixer. Many modern pizzerias use this type of mixer. It's more powerful than a regular stand mixer, with a wide beater that massages the dough. The whole bowl rotates for superior kneading, providing better pull and action. It also handles twice the quantity of most standard mixers.

Pizza Crisper Pan: These steel pans have little holes for air circulation, resulting in a crispy pizza crust. The dough doesn't get caught in the holes. I use this the most for any flat pizza. You don't need a pizza stone when you use this crisper on the bottom rack of your oven.

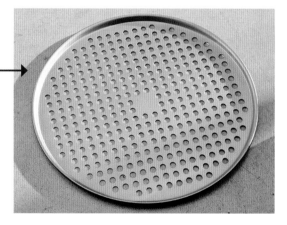

Buy 14- or 16-inch rounds, preferably not nonstick (nonstick pans used in high heat have a shorter life). Measure your oven first to make sure that a 16-inch pan will fit. Some pans have thick rolled edges that keep the pan from warping, which is a good thing because you'll be using high heat.

Pizza Screen: This pan also works wonders for any flat pizza. The aluminum wire mesh provides maximum airflow, which results in a crispy pizza crust. Very little comes between the dough and the heat, which is what you want. Buy 14- or 16-inch rounds, but measure your oven first to make sure a 16-inch pan will fit.

You don't need a pizza stone when you use this screen on the bottom rack of your oven.

I always spray the screen first with a nonstick cooking spray, but every once and a while the dough catches in the wire, so it can be a little hard to clean. It can also warp after a while from continued use at high temperatures.

To bake more than one pizza at a meal, invest in at least two of these pizza pans—either the crisper or the screen or different sizes of one kind, so you don't have to wait for a hot pan to cool down. They're inexpensive and you will love the crispy, brown crust.

Baking Steel: If you want to go high-tech with a superior product, try placing your shaped pizza dough on a baking steel. Get one that's 14 or 16 inches in diameter and $1/4$ inch thick. It's pricey and heavy, so this is an optional tool, but the slab will even out the heat in the oven, eliminating hot spots and producing a crispy, browned pizza. It also gets hot faster than a pizza stone.

Pizza Stone: I don't use a pizza stone much because I find that putting a pizza on the bottom rack of a hot oven, on a pizza screen or pan, makes it nice and crispy. Many ovens have hot spots, however, and placing a pizza stone on the bottom of your oven is a good way to even out the heat. You can leave it in all the time. If you really like using a stone, by all means cook your pie on it. Pizza stones absorb moisture and crisp the pizza. But if you have not bought a stone yet, I'd buy the screen and crisper pans instead.

Terra-Cotta Tiles: If you want a less expensive version of a pizza stone, buy 6 by 6-inch unglazed terra-cotta tiles from a building supply store. Just be sure they are all natural, with no finish or ingredients that will leach into the pizza. Line the oven floor with six of them and you will find that the oven heats more evenly. This is an optional project for DIY types.

Sicilian Pizza Pan: This is the authentic way to make the Sicilian pizzas in Chapter 5, and worth the investment if you intend to make big and beautiful focaccialike pizzas regularly. This 15 by 15-inch pan has 1-inch-deep sides and a bottom that keeps the crust crispy because it's made of steel. It's easier to make the Sicilian pizzas in this pan than in a half sheet pan, because it's the right size. It's an optional purchase but one you will enjoy. Wash and dry this square pan immediately after use or it can rust on you.

Half Sheet Pan: Usually made of aluminum, these pans are used for the Grandma and Grandpa Sicilian pizzas (pages 88 and 90). These are for the rectangular pizzas you purchase by the piece in pizzerias and Italian bakeries, the kind that sit in the pan all day. The pans are usually about 18 x $12^{1}/_{2}$ inches, with 1-inch-high sides. Buy a heavy one that will not warp, if you do not already own a similar sheet pan. They're also good for roasting vegetables.

Deep-Dish Pizza Pans: I like to use deep-dish pans made of steel or terra-cotta stone to make an authentic deep-dish pie. Their thick walls slow down the heat so the outside of the crust doesn't burn. Slower, more even cooking makes your pizzas taste better.

Deep-dish pans come in 12- and 14-inch diameters, and I use both in this cookbook. I prefer not to use nonstick pans, because they have a shorter shelf life when used in high heat. Steel cake pans are too thin, but can be used in a pinch if you have one that is the right diameter.

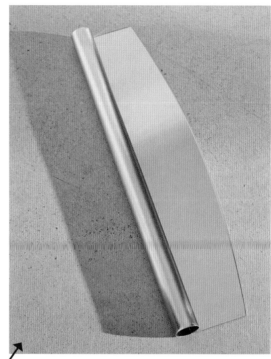

Pizza Cutters: My favorite cutter is the large mezzaluna, or rocker knife. Mine is 16 inches long. It has a rocking motion that leverages your weight to cut through the pizza cleanly. It takes two hands to operate. Its advantage is that it won't dislodge the toppings.

Rolling wheels push the toppings around, especially if the wheel is dull. Buy a good one—they only cost around twenty dollars. Plastic rolling wheels come in handy when you're cutting pizza in a pan, because they are less likely to damage the pan.

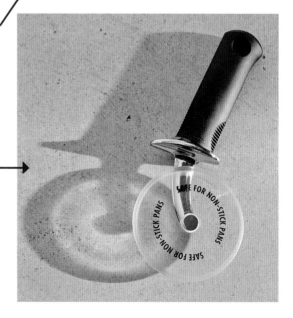

Pizza Scissors: It never occurred to me to cut a pizza with scissors until I bought some 12-inch shears specifically designed for the task. This is a convenient way to cut a pizza cleanly, straight through it versus making a sawing motion with a knife or cutter that tears the pizza. If you like gadgets in your kitchen, this is a fun one to try.

Pizza Peel: Most cutting boards aren't big enough to hold a 14- or 16-inch-wide pizza, so a big pizza peel, one made of bamboo or wood, comes in handy. I'm not talking about the long-handled kind that pizzaiolos use to take a pizza out of a wood-burning oven. This kind has a short handle made for holding with one hand. You can put the pizza pan right on the wood and it will not burn, but the main reason to get it is because you need a big enough space to cut and serve the pizza, and a peel works beautifully. I like the 16-inch round ones.

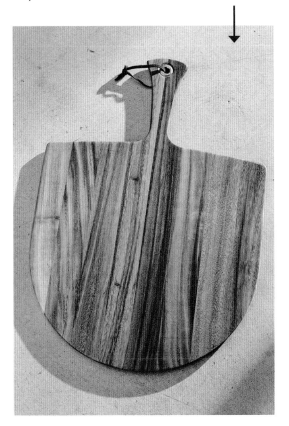

Heavy-Duty Oven Mitts: Your pizza will cook in a 500°F oven, and it will be molten when it's done. Heavy-duty oven mitts let you grab the pizza without worrying about burning yourself. Get mitts with an outer fabric that resists scorching and burning. These are way better than trying to remove the pizza with tiny 6- or 8-inch squares of cloth.

Dough Docker: Not essential, but fun to have. Made in the shape of a paint roller with prongs sticking out, it's best for the super-thin, cracker-like St. Louis–style dough (page 70). The prongs punch into the dough, allowing gas to release while it cooks so the thin crust stays flat.

TECHNIQUE

Making pizza is sensuous. There's the pleasure of gently stretching out silky, supple dough that's so easy to handle that your shaped dough goes on the pan in a few moments. You apply the toppings like an artist, enjoying the beautiful patterns and colors on the round canvas. You smell the pizza cooking, that savory baking aroma that envelops your kitchen. Then, you remove the pie and marvel at how it looks, so brown and crisp and caramelized, the colors darker but still vibrant. And then you eat a slice, enjoying the spongy crackle of the crust and the luscious toppings that make you sigh with pleasure.

That experience is what keeps me making pizza, and what I hope will inspire you to make the recipes in this book. This next part gives you an overview of what to expect when making pizzas, and provides a few tricks of the trade to help you make the dough, stretch it out, top it, bake it, and even cut it.

Pizzas can't be assembled in advance and refrigerated. But you can prepare ingredients beforehand so it just takes a few minutes to assemble a pizza and bake it. Later in the chapter I'll discuss how to plan ahead.

Choosing a Pizza Dough

A great pizza begins with a spectacular crust. You probably have a favorite crust, but I hope you'll branch out and enjoy the variety. The following is how the different doughs pan out.

NAPLES	Soft and crispy, this tender dough is low in gluten because of its special 00 flour. It takes two days to make, starting with a poolish (fermented dough) for added flavor and complexity.
NEW YORK	Stretchy and strong, with a yeasty flavor, this dough is fast and easy to make. It's used for most pizza across the country. It can be crunchy or soft, depending on how long it bakes.
SICILIAN	Soft, fluffy, and oily, with a thin veneer of crispy crust, this dough must be baked in a heavy pan because it is so soft.
SOURDOUGH	Tangy, chewy, and strong, sourdough crusts are filled with large air bubbles. It takes five days to make this dough, but once you try it, you'll be hooked, and your starter will be waiting for you in the fridge.
STUFFED	A strong dough built for extra hold, with added flavor from cornmeal, stuffed dough can be stretchy and works well for filled pizzas.
CORN FLOUR	Sweet and corny, this soft, delicate dough has a fluffy interior with a thin veneer of crispy crust.
WHOLE WHEAT	A strong dough with the power to hold many toppings, this crust has a nutty flavor and comes out of the oven dark brown.
GLUTEN-FREE	Made from a batter prebaked into a round, this dough is then baked again when topped as a crust. A variety of sweet flours make it crunchy, porous, crispy, and tender. It's worth trying even if you can eat gluten.

If You Want to Switch Crusts

What if you like one kind of crust and another kind of topping—can you change it? Absolutely. The most important consideration is the amount of topping—don't add too much, which can sink the more porous and softer crusts.

NAPLES	Go light on the toppings, as it is softer and more delicate than other doughs.
NEW YORK	This is an all-purpose dough, so you can top it with anything you like. If you don't have time to make sourdough, this dough is your easiest alternative.
SICILIAN	Keep it in its intended pan because of its softness, but cover it with whatever you like. Because it makes a large ball, you might need to make 1½ times the amount of topping.
SOURDOUGH	This strong dough can take just about any topping. It is a good choice if you like extra tang in your dough.
STUFFED	Experiment with different fillings. It can stretch and hold many fillings without breaking, so keep it for its intended purpose.
CORN FLOUR	Because the dough is porous, some toppings could soak in, so stick to the less saucy ones. It pairs well with tangy toppings and earthy vegetables. Also keep in mind that the dough ball is a little smaller than others.
WHOLE WHEAT	This dough is porous and breadlike on the inside. Because it's so firm, it can handle any topping.
GLUTEN-FREE	Porous and crispy, this dough works best with pizza toppings that are not too wet or heavy.

Making and Shaping the Dough

Using the Right Equipment: A stand mixer is essential (each dough recipe has directions for kneading in a stand mixer) because the doughs take some time to create, and stand mixers handle the job well.

The doughs are too big to fit in a food processor, so if you don't have a stand mixer, make a dough by hand. Just mix the dough together with a wooden spoon in a large bowl. Gather up the dough and place it on a floured countertop. Push and fold the dough for the time listed in the recipe. Keep working the dough until it passes the windowpane test (see the Naples-style, New York–style, and sourdough dough recipes for an explanation).

Letting the Dough Rest: You will see in the dough recipes that my technique calls for combining the ingredients on low speed until they form a rough mass, without the salt. Then you turn off the mixer and let the dough rest for about 10 minutes. This is called autolyse, when the strands of gluten absorb liquids. A short rest before kneading will improve your dough.

Measuring the Flour: Many pizza doughs come out too runny or too stiff even when you are positive that you have followed the instructions exactly. The issue can be how you measure the flour. I use the scoop-and-level method with my 1/4-cup measure, dipping it into the flour and scooping it into my 1-cup measure. Then I level it off with the back of a butter knife. I don't pack down the flour or tap the cup on the counter to level the flour.

Using the Right Flour: Some crusts don't work if you use the wrong type of wheat flour. Stronger doughs—the New York, Naples, and sourdough—require unbleached bread flour because the higher gluten content gives them a good chew. The Sicilian, stuffed, corn flour, and whole wheat doughs all use unbleached all-purpose flour because their crusts are softer. The Naples pizza has a silky dough when you use Italian 00 flour.

Brand-name flours may cost a few pennies more, but it's worth the expense. Not all flour is the same, nor does it have the same attributes. For unbleached all-purpose flour, I prefer Ceresota or King Arthur flours. At about 12 percent gluten, you get a little less stretch in the dough and a softer crust. I usually mix this flour with others to create different crusts. I also use King Arthur unbleached bread flour, a high-gluten flour with about 14 percent protein, to give pizzas that irresistible chewy crust.

Proofing Doughs for Several Hours: The best way to make great pizza dough is to let it proof (rest and rise) in the refrigerator for at least 12 hours and up to 72 hours. The yeast has lots of time to act on the carbohydrates, creating the carbon dioxide bubbles that make the dough rise. Otherwise the dough will be flatter, have less sheen, and it won't brown as well. It's worth the time and requires a little planning. It's not extra work because the dough just sits there.

The Right Yeast: Use active dry yeast, sometimes referred to as "baker's yeast." It is a live culture that is dehydrated and used to make doughs rise for breads, rolls, and pizza. I find it easier to use, easier to find, and just as effective as fresh cake yeast.

Letting Dough Come to Room Temperature: Pizza dough needs to come to room temperature so it can start rising immediately in the oven. Cold dough won't rise well in the oven. Cold dough is also harder to stretch out because it snaps back. But don't let the dough sit out much longer than an hour, because soft dough is hard to handle, and sometimes it can fall through the holes in a pizza pan or screen.

Handling Dough with Care: Be gentle with your dough when it's time to shape it. Invert the bowl and let it fall onto a floured counter. Dust the dough with flour and gently pat the flour onto it. Then pick up the dough and hold it gently. Let it fall over your hands, then move your hands apart to stretch it to the diameter you want.

I hardly ever roll out the crusts in this book. They don't need it. Besides, doing so could crush out the gas that makes them light and crispy, and you won't get a good rim. Exceptions are the whole wheat Grilled Pizza Calamari (page 164), Imo's Deluxe (page 70) with a crackery crust, and the Punctuated Equilibrium (page 163) flatbread pizza. When you flatten the dough with a rolling pin, it will stay flat in the oven and on the grill.

Most of the time you will prepare the dough on the floured counter and then transfer it to the pan. You want to avoid pressing the dough on the pan, especially when using the screen and pizza crisper pans, which will lead to dough squishing into the holes and possibly sticking to the pan.

When you've shaped your dough, look for holes. If you find one, just pinch it together to repair the dough; otherwise, the sauce will come between the pan and the crust and create a pizza that sticks to the pan. The sauce might even drip onto the bottom of the oven and create a smoky mess. I put a thick layer of foil on the bottom of the oven, to catch the drips and make any mess easier to remove.

Buying Dough: If you're in a hurry, buy fresh pizza dough from a supermarket or pizzeria. It's not worth buying frozen pizza or bread dough, though, because in the time it takes you to defrost it, you can make your own fresh dough, which will taste better.

BUILDING THE PIZZA

Topping the pizza is a matter of mastering how much of each ingredient to use. It's best not to overload a pizza, no matter what the ingredient. Build your pie with care and artistry. The following are some guidelines.

Sauce: There's a limit to how much sauce a pizza will hold. Most 14-inch pizzas hold 1½ cups of sauce, maximum. I pour red sauce into the middle of the shaped dough and spread it with the bottom of the ladle, in concentric circles, just like a pizzaiolo. You can also just spread it from side to side with a rubber spatula or the back of a spoon.

Toppings: Spread out your toppings evenly. Don't pile them in the middle because the ingredients will naturally slide there anyway, as the rim develops and pushes them in. Create little pockets of flavors and textures by spooning small mounds of thick sauces like pesto or bundles of ingredients like folded cured meats all over. This way you get different tastes and textures in each bite, instead of every bite tasting the same. The pizzas look prettier too.

Cheese: Create an even blanket. The amount of cheese is generally 2 cups or less. There *is* such a thing as too much cheese! It can result in a greasy pizza where toppings slide around. Some toppings work best on top of the cheese, because they need crisping or browning. Bits of sausage, salumi, and bacon work well this way because the edges caramelize.

A Word about Mozzarella

Many of the pizzas in this cookbook contain fresh or dried mozzarella, a mild Italian cheese that anchors toppings to their crusts. Fresh mozzarella is sold in balls, and dried mozzarella comes in blocks or pre-shredded in a plastic bag. Here's more about each type and when to use them.

FRESH MOZZARELLA	Called *fior de latte,* it comes in milky white balls. It has not been aged, so it has a high moisture content and tastes like fresh milk. You can find this cheese in plastic containers in the deli section of your market. Fresh mozzarella works best on strong crusts like sourdough and New York. Its wetness will add moisture to your pizza, though, so avoid combining it with toppings like roasted zucchini or tomato. I slice or tear balls of fresh mozzarella and place the pieces on the pizza about an inch or two from one another because the cheese will spread out as it cooks.
AGED MOZZARELLA	This comes in block form or pre-shredded. This is the part-skim cheese most pizzerias use to hold other ingredients in place, and when the recipe calls for shredded mozzarella, this is what you use. (Occasionally you can find a block of whole milk cheese, which is softer, richer, and moister. It also results in less stretch.) A block of mozzarella gives you more cheese for your money than pre-shredded cheese. Use a box grater or a food processor to shred it into thin ribbons for ease of melting. Pre-shredded mozzarella is a great convenience product and I confess to using it many times. But one drawback is the anti-caking additive. It does not change the taste of the cheese but I find that it shortens the stretch. Pre-shredded cheese does not promote long cheese pulls from hot pizza, one of the great pleasures of a gooey slice.

Baking and Serving Your Pizza

Now that you know how to make a great-looking pie, it needs to go into the oven to crisp and brown. Almost all the pizzas in this cookbook (except the grilled and gluten-free pies) bake for 15 to 20 minutes at the lowest rack, about an inch from the oven floor, at 500°F. The oven needs to preheat for 30 minutes to reach this high, stable temperature or the pizza will bake on top but not on the bottom. The bottom of a pizza crisps beautifully once the oven is hot. You've probably experienced soggy dough in the middle of a pizza. This is how you banish it forever.

When your pizza has rested for 5 minutes, you will transfer it to a wooden peel or board. Cutting into a metal pan with a metal knife will scratch the pan, so use a plastic pizza slicer or a serrated knife, and press lightly. Exceptions are the deep-dish and Sicilian pizzas, where you can keep the pizzas in the pan and cut out a slice at a time.

Working in Advance

Great pizzas take a little planning. Since the doughs rest overnight in the refrigerator, make it worth your time and double or triple the amount of dough you make. Freeze the extras for up to 3 months, and defrost them a day ahead. Make the dough up to 3 days in advance. An extra day or two in the refrigerator helps the dough develop flavor and volume.

The red sauces come together easily and need time for flavors to develop, so I make them the night before too. If you need to get a pizza on the table in a hurry, shred the cheese, cut up the vegetables, or cook the meat the day before. The recipes are written using *mise en place,* a French term that means to get all the ingredients ready first. I put them all on the counter in small containers, which makes it easy to assemble the pizzas quickly.

Now that you've learned about the basics of making pizza, please bake and eat these world-class pizzas from all over America. The next chapter lists recipes for toppings and sauces used most in this cookbook, and then it's on to the pizzas, dough by dough.

Chapter 2

SAUCES and TOPPINGS

How do you judge a great pizza? First comes the dough, and a close second is the sauce. This chapter contains sauces used on pizzas throughout the book, including three tomato sauces, two of which are uncooked.

So many pizzas are all about the red sauce. I make three kinds: the Chunky Tomato Sauce, New York–Style Pizza Sauce, and Cooked Tomato Sauce. Chunky Tomato Sauce is a little sweet, with tomato bits for texture and flavor, and small amounts of fresh basil and garlic. It's good for deep-dish pizzas and pies with a strong dough, such as sourdough, to hold the heavy water content of the sauce. It's the easiest sauce to make: just mix a few ingredients together in a bowl and let it rest to build flavor.

The New York–Style Pizza Sauce is smooth, pureed with herbs and oil, with a roasted garlic flavor. Romano cheese thickens the sauce so water does not release when the pizza cooks. The flavor is strong, so you can use a little less on crusts. It's best for New York Dough pizzas, keeping them flexible and chewy.

Cooked Tomato Sauce is thick as well, made with tomato puree and tomato paste. This sauce is darker in color due to its dried herbs. This thick sauce is best for thin-crust pizzas. Because it is not wet, thin crusts won't get soggy.

Other sauces in this chapter are a pesto with almonds brightened with parsley and a cream sauce that can become a cheese sauce. I've also included a few vegetable toppings that appear regularly throughout the book, and one baked chicken breast. The great advantage of all these sauces and toppings is that they come together quickly and easily. You'll be rewarded with intense flavors that don't require much effort.

If you want to work in advance, make many of these recipes up to three days ahead and refrigerate until ready. All make enough for one pizza. Don't try to freeze the red sauces because the tomato breaks down and becomes watery.

CHUNKY TOMATO SAUCE

1 cup diced plum tomatoes with juice (preferably canned San Marzanos)

2 tablespoons tomato paste

1 clove garlic, minced

1 tablespoon extra-virgin olive oil

4 big fresh basil leaves, chopped

1 teaspoon sugar

1/2 teaspoon salt

1/2 teaspoon freshly ground black pepper

I use this zesty tomato sauce on many pizzas because it blends so well with different flavors and adds a shiny bright red base. It only takes a few minutes to make and the taste is great. You can make this sauce up to three days in advance. Store in an airtight container in the refrigerator.

MAKES ABOUT 1 1/2 CUPS, ENOUGH FOR ONE (14- OR 16-INCH) PIZZA

Mix all the ingredients together in a medium bowl. Let the sauce sit for 1 hour, either on the counter or in the refrigerator, to allow the flavors to meld.

COOKED TOMATO SAUCE

1 tablespoon extra-virgin olive oil

2 cloves garlic, minced

1/2 teaspoon dried basil

1/2 teaspoon dried oregano

1/4 teaspoon dried thyme

1 teaspoon salt

1/2 teaspoon freshly ground black pepper

1 cup canned tomato puree or sauce

2 tablespoons tomato paste

This spicy tomato sauce with classic flavorings of dried basil and oregano is cooked, making it rich and thick. It's the perfect consistency for any type of pizza, but I especially like it on New York–style crusts because it goes so well with a chewy crust. I prefer using tomato puree, though you can also use tomato sauce, which is flavored. If you use the sauce, you will probably need less salt. You can make this sauce up to three days in advance. Store in an airtight container in the refrigerator.

MAKES 1 CUP, ENOUGH FOR ONE (14- OR 16-INCH) PIZZA

Heat the olive oil in a small saucepan over medium heat. Toss in the garlic and stir with a wooden spoon for 30 seconds. Add the basil, oregano, thyme, salt, and pepper and cook for about 30 seconds, stirring continuously. Add the tomato puree and paste. Mix thoroughly and cook over medium-low heat for 10 minutes, stirring occasionally.

NEW YORK–STYLE PIZZA SAUCE

2   tablespoons extra-virgin olive oil

2   cloves garlic

1/2 cup canned Roma tomatoes, diced

2   tablespoons tomato paste

1   tablespoon chopped fresh basil leaves

1   teaspoon sugar

1/2 teaspoon salt

1/2 teaspoon freshly ground black pepper

1   tablespoon grated Pecorino Romano

Before I met some New Yorkers who make pizzas every day, I had never thought of frying my garlic to get a mellow roasted flavor in my sauce. I also hadn't thought of adding sharp Pecorino Romano cheese to bolster its flavor. This rich tomato sauce has character. It says, "Hey, I'm walkin' here!" You can make this sauce up to three days in advance. Store in an airtight container in the refrigerator.

MAKES ABOUT 3/4 CUP, ENOUGH FOR ONE (14- OR 16-INCH) PIZZA

Heat the olive oil in a small saucepan over medium heat. Add the garlic cloves and cook until they are golden brown, about 2 minutes. Remove from the heat and let cool.

Transfer the garlic and the oil from the pan to a food processor fitted with the metal blade. Add the tomatoes, tomato paste, basil, sugar, salt, and pepper and puree until smooth. Add the grated Romano and pulse to combine.

Let the sauce sit for 1 hour, either on the counter or in the refrigerator, to allow the flavors to meld.

PESTO SAUCE

1 cup packed fresh basil leaves (from about 2 bunches)

2 cloves garlic, peeled

1/2 cup extra-virgin olive oil

1/2 cup packed fresh flat-leaf parsley (from about 1/2 bunch)

1/4 cup grated Parmigiano Reggiano

1/4 cup chopped almonds, preferably unsalted

1 teaspoon salt

1/2 teaspoon freshly ground black pepper

I haven't found a jarred pesto that I prefer to homemade. It takes only about five minutes to whip up this sauce, provided you have a food processor or a good blender. If not, you can always mash up the ingredients in a mortar and pestle. Roasted chicken and roasted vegetables like broccoli, zucchini, onions, and peppers work well as pizza toppings for this pesto sauce. You can make this sauce up to three days in advance. Store in an airtight container in the refrigerator. You can also freeze it for up to ninety days in a freezer bag, but it will darken in color.

MAKES 3/4 CUP, ENOUGH FOR ONE (14- OR 16-INCH) PIZZA

Put all the ingredients in a food processor and puree until smooth.

ALFREDO SAUCE

2 tablespoons unsalted butter

3 tablespoons unbleached all-purpose flour

1 1/2 cups whole milk

1 teaspoon salt

1/8 teaspoon ground white pepper

1 bay leaf

1/2 teaspoon hot pepper sauce

1/8 teaspoon ground nutmeg

This creamy sauce has lots of flavor and tastes great on pizza topped with chicken, shrimp, lobster, or salmon. Add Swiss cheese to make a classic Mornay sauce. Add Parmigiano Reggiano to make it sharper. You can make this sauce up to four days in advance. Store in an airtight container in the refrigerator.

MAKES 1 1/2 CUPS, ENOUGH FOR ONE (14- OR 16-INCH) PIZZA

Melt the butter in a small saucepan over medium-low heat. Add the flour and stir continuously with a wooden spoon until a smooth paste forms, about 2 minutes. Add the milk, salt, pepper, bay leaf, hot sauce, and nutmeg. Cook, stirring often to prevent scalding on the bottom. The sauce will thicken in 4 to 6 minutes. Remove from the heat and let cool for about 10 minutes. Discard the bay leaf.

HERBED OLIVE OIL

2 tablespoons extra-virgin olive oil

1 clove garlic, minced

1/2 teaspoon dried thyme

1/2 teaspoon dried basil

1/2 teaspoon dried oregano

I use this infused olive oil instead of sauce to create herby garlic tastiness that amps up the flavor of pizzas. I spread it on the shaped dough before adding the toppings. You could also use this oil to sauté shrimp or chicken breast, or to baste grilled meats.

MAKES 3 TABLESPOONS, ENOUGH FOR ONE (14 OR 16-INCH) PIZZA

Combine all the ingredients in a medium bowl. Use immediately or store in the refrigerator for up to 3 days.

ROASTED TOMATOES

3 medium tomatoes

2 tablespoons extra-virgin olive oil

1/2 teaspoon salt

1/2 teaspoon freshly ground black pepper

The rich, sweet flavor of tomatoes amplifies when roasted. It only takes a few minutes but the wallop of intense flavor makes it seem like they took all day. These are so much better than slices of fresh tomato on your pizza, where the flavor gets washed out and the tomato turns to water. Make these roasted tomatoes as needed, as they will not keep.

MAKES 12 WEDGES, ENOUGH FOR ONE (14- OR 16-INCH) PIZZA

Preheat the oven to 400°F.

Cut the tomatoes into quarters and remove the cores from each. Toss the tomatoes, olive oil, salt, and pepper on a half sheet pan.

Bake for 15 minutes, until soft and lightly browned. Let cool for 5 minutes before using.

ROASTED RED PEPPER STRIPS

1 red bell pepper

$1/2$ teaspoon extra-virgin olive oil

These colorful, tasty strips of red pepper give pizzas an instant lift. You can refrigerate these strips for up to two weeks in an airtight container. Don't put them in the freezer, though, as they will turn to mush.

MAKES ABOUT $1/2$ CUP, ENOUGH FOR ONE (14- OR 16-INCH) PIZZA

Turn on the broiler and move the oven rack to the top shelf. Put the whole pepper on a cookie sheet and place it under the broiler.

Within a few minutes you'll hear the pepper crackle, and a toasty aroma will come off the skin. Turn the pepper with tongs to ensure all sides get direct heat, 2 to 3 minutes for each side. The pepper will be charred completely black.

Transfer the charred pepper to a bowl and cover with plastic wrap. After 5 minutes, the steam will loosen the skin and make it easier to peel. Take the pepper to the sink and put a strainer under it before you gently peel off the black skin. Pull off the stem and remove the core and seeds. Give the pepper a slight rinse with cool water.

Slice the roasted pepper into thin strips and place in a small bowl. Toss with the olive oil. If not using immediately, seal in a plastic bag and refrigerate.

ROASTED GARLIC CLOVES

12 cloves garlic, peeled   Pinch of salt

1 teaspoon extra-virgin olive oil

These little nuggets are like flavor bombs. When you find one in a pizza, it will fill your mouth with a rich, buttery taste. You can add roasted garlic to any pizza when you want to boost the flavor. I also like to throw them into salads.

Many stores sell peeled fresh garlic cloves—a real time-saver. Do not confuse the raw garlic with pickled, chopped, or crushed garlic.

I roast these in water, with just a bit of olive oil, which keeps the garlic cloves soft but not so soft that they loose their shape when cooked on a pizza. If you roast the cloves in olive oil only, they become too crispy and dried out.

You can refrigerate the garlic in the liquid in an airtight container for up to two weeks.

MAKES 12 GARLIC CLOVES, ENOUGH FOR ONE (14- OR 16-INCH) PIZZA

Preheat the oven or a toaster oven to 400°F.

Place the garlic, olive oil, and salt in a small baking dish, such as a mini loaf pan, ramekin, or custard dish. Add only enough water to cover. Bake for about 1 hour, or until the cloves are browned in places and soft.

ROASTED ZUCCHINI

2 medium zucchini

2 tablespoons extra-virgin olive oil

1/2 teaspoon salt

1/2 teaspoon freshly ground black pepper

Pre-roasted zucchini slices add a rich mouthfeel to pizzas. I like to use both green zucchini and yellow squash to create a pretty design—but using one or the other works fine too. Make this zucchini as needed, as it will not keep.

MAKES ABOUT 1 CUP, ENOUGH FOR ONE (14- OR 16-INCH) PIZZA

Preheat the oven to 400°F.

Slice the ends off the zucchini and slice them into 1/4-inch-thick rounds. Toss the zucchini, olive oil, salt, and pepper on a sheet pan and spread out the slices in a single layer. Roast for 15 minutes, until browned and soft.

SAUTÉED MUSHROOMS

1/4 pound white button or cremini mushrooms, thinly sliced (about 2 cups)

1 1/2 teaspoons extra-virgin olive oil

1/4 teaspoon salt

Pinch of freshly ground black pepper

Raw mushrooms dry out on top of a pizza, so sautéing them first is essential. Sautéing them releases their flavor and makes them tender and juicy. Best of all, it only takes a few minutes. You can make these up to three days in advance. Store in an airtight container in the refrigerator.

MAKES ABOUT 1 CUP, ENOUGH FOR 1 (14- OR 16-INCH) PIZZA

Wash the mushrooms right before cooking. Rinse them well while rubbing them with your hands. Pat them dry with paper towels.

Heat the olive oil in a small skillet over medium-high heat. Add the mushrooms and sauté until soft, about 3 minutes. Season with the salt and pepper.

ROASTED CHICKEN BREAST

1	boneless, skinless chicken breast, about 8 ounces	Salt and freshly ground black pepper
1	teaspoon extra-virgin olive oil	

I like to put thin strips of roasted chicken on pizzas. Strips are easier to eat than chunks, which fall off. In this recipe, you partially cook the breast, as it will continue to cook on the pizza. You could make more and freeze them for up to ninety days. Or make them up to three days ahead and refrigerate in an airtight container or resealable plastic bag.

MAKES 1 CHICKEN BREAST, ENOUGH FOR ONE (14- OR 16-INCH) PIZZA

Preheat the oven to 400°F.

Place the chicken breast in a small pan. Coat the chicken with the olive oil and sprinkle generously with salt and pepper. Bake for 15 minutes. The chicken will be only partially cooked. Let cool for 10 minutes. If using immediately, cut the chicken into thin slices. Store the breast whole if you are making it ahead, so it doesn't dry out.

Chapter 3

NAPLES-STYLE PIZZAS

The birthplace of pizza is Naples, Italy. While yeast-raised flatbreads were baked all over the world, it was in Naples where tomato and then cheeses hit the crust. In the seventeenth century, Neapolitans realized that tomatoes were not poisonous as people originally thought, and began roasting the plentiful fruit on dough in wood ovens all over the city. And it was not on just any dough, but dough made with doppio zero ("00") flour, which is extremely fine, like talcum powder. It is also very low in proteins, which gives pizza dough extra silkiness.

It took nearly one hundred years more for an enterprising young Neapolitan pizzaiolo, Raffaele Esposito, while making a pizza for Queen Margherita, to put cheese on the tomatoes. Thin-crust pizza with cheese, tomatoes, and basil—the colors of the Italian flag—was here to stay.

Fast-forward to America, where Italian immigrants Giovanni and Gennero Bruno brought their dough to America in 1903 to introduce the Neapolitan pizza. At first, they sold their pizzas on the street. Then Gennaro

...mbardi opened America's first pizzeria in 1905 in Manhattan. Naples-style pizza became wildly popular, and this love affair continues today, with cities and towns all over the United States boasting Naples-style pizzerias equipped with coal- or wood-burning ovens.

The most traditional Neapolitan pizza appears on page 45, where it's supplemented with capicola, a cured ham. Meanwhile, many pizza restaurants across the country offer more than the standard tomato and cheese pie, topping the crispy Naples dough with lobster (on the East Coast), white beans and asparagus (on the West Coast), and other creative combinations in between.

The Naples dough takes a little time to produce, but not more effort. The night before, you make a pre-ferment called a poolish by mixing equal parts water and flour plus a little yeast. It takes just a few minutes to make, and creates dough that has already undergone fermentation. This process increases the flavor and complexity of the finished crust. Traditionally, it's made with only four ingredients: flour, water, yeast, and salt. This produces a lean dough without oil or sugar, made to bake quickly at temperatures as high as 1,000°F. For home ovens, which bake at half the temperature, I've added a little honey and oil to make the crust moist and crispy.

All the pizzas in this chapter have a puffy crust around the rim, so leave a 1-inch border of dough bare around the edge when adding toppings.

NAPLES-STYLE PIZZA DOUGH

FOR THE POOLISH

$1/2$ cup plus
2 tablespoons
unbleached bread
flour

$1/8$ teaspoon active
dry yeast

$1/2$ cup plus
2 tablespoons
water

FOR THE DOUGH

$1/2$ cup unbleached
bread flour, plus
more for dusting

$1/2$ cup plus
2 tablespoons
Italian 00 flour

1 tablespoon extra-
virgin olive oil,
plus 1 teaspoon for
the bowl

1 teaspoon honey

1 teaspoon active
dry yeast

$1/4$ cup water

$1/2$ teaspoon salt

Nonstick cooking spray

This dough makes a spongy crust with a crispy top. It incorporates a poolish, a dough starter that gives the crust extra flavor and character. Make the poolish the night before and leave it to ferment on your counter for at least twelve hours. The next morning, mix it into the dough, refrigerate it, and by evening you'll have dough that's easy to handle and ready to bake.

In this recipe, I combine Italian 00 flour (also called Caputo 00 flour) with bread flour, which provides strength and structure to the dough. The 00 flour is so soft that it is best used in combination with another strong gluten flour.

It is worth the time and effort to use this 00 flour, as it gives a silkiness and authentic texture to the Naples dough. Look for it in Italian specialty stores or online. If you cannot find it, use unbleached bread flour. The dough will be less silky, and you may have to add about 2 tablespoons more water because the bread flour is more absorbent.

MAKES ENOUGH DOUGH FOR 1 (14-INCH) PIZZA CRUST

Make the Poolish: Mix the flour, yeast, and water in a small bowl. Cover with plastic wrap and let sit overnight at room temperature, about 12 hours. The poolish will bubble as fermentation takes place. When it is ready, it will teem with millions of living yeast cells.

Make the Dough: Scrape the poolish into the bowl of a stand mixer fitted with the dough hook. Add the bread and 00 flours, 1 tablespoon of the oil, the honey, yeast, and water. Mix together on low speed until a dough ball forms.

Turn off the mixer and let the dough rest for about 10 minutes. Add the salt. Knead the dough on medium speed for 15 minutes. When the dough is ready, it will be wet, sticky, and elastic. To test elasticity, hold a 1-inch piece between your fingers and stretch the dough. This is called making a windowpane. The dough should look like stretched-out bubblegum (see page 20 for a photo). If not, knead for another 5 minutes and test again. Keep kneading until the dough passes the test, up to 30 minutes more.

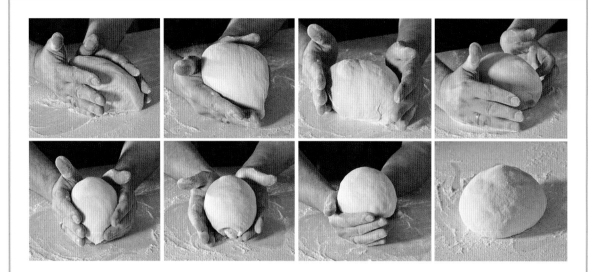

Pour the remaining 1 teaspoon olive oil into a large bowl. Wet your hands with water, shape the dough into a ball, and place it in the bowl. Turn the dough to coat it with oil. This prevents a crust from forming on its surface as it rises. Cover the bowl with plastic wrap and let the dough rise in the refrigerator for about 12 hours. It will double in width when ready. Rest the dough on the counter until it comes to room temperature, about 1 hour.

Get the Dough in Shape

STRETCH THE DOUGH Lightly flour a clean, dry countertop. Gently place the round of dough on your counter. Do not knead or press on it. Instead, let it settle. Dust the top with flour.

Make dimples in the dough with your fingertips by pressing down in the middle to stretch it out. Move the dough around in a circle as you press down with your fingertips. A 1-inch rim will be created naturally. Press your fingertips along the inside of the rim, moving in a circle. Place your hands on the dough, fingers up against the rim, and push out while turning in a circle. Add more flour, if necessary, to ensure the dough slides easily.

Finish stretching the dough by sliding your open hands underneath it and picking it up. Let the dough fall around your hands to stretch it. Keep your hands along the edges, rather than in the middle. Stretch it to 14 inches in diameter.

HAND-TOSSING TECHNIQUE You can hand-toss any of the pizza doughs in this chapter if you like. Pick up the dough and, with your palms down, drape the dough over the knuckles of both hands. Toss the dough a few inches into the air and put a little spin on it to rotate the dough. Do this several times and keep the dough close to your hands. Don't throw it up into the air. The dough should be thin in the center with a ring around the edge, 14 inches in diameter.

PLACE THE DOUGH ON THE PAN OR SCREEN Spray a 14-inch pizza pan with nonstick cooking spray and place it next to the shaped dough. Slide the shaped dough onto the pan. Reshape as necessary. If you've hand-tossed the dough, spray the pan before you start and transfer the shaped dough to the pan. Your Naples-style dough is now ready for pizza toppings.

SPRING LAMB SAUSAGE PIZZA

Lamb ▲ Eggplant ▲ Kalamata Olives

Naples-Style Pizza Dough (page 39)

Roasted Garlic Cloves (page 33)

3   lamb sausages (about 12 ounces total)

1   medium eggplant (about 1¹/2 pounds), cut into 1-inch cubes

Zest and juice of 1 lemon

4   tablespoons extra-virgin olive oil

1   cup dry white wine, such as Pinot Grigio

3   ounces Pecorino Romano, grated (¹/4 cup)

1   cup shredded mozzarella

2   ounces feta, crumbled (¹/2 cup)

12 pitted kalamata olives, halved

1   teaspoon dried oregano

1   tablespoon chopped fresh flat-leaf parsley

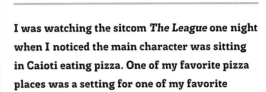

I was watching the sitcom *The League* one night when I noticed the main character was sitting in Caioti eating pizza. One of my favorite pizza places was a setting for one of my favorite shows!

Maybe it was this Spring Lamb Pizza that brought them to film there, or maybe it's because Caioti is a destination pizzeria created by Ed LaDou, a pizza master responsible for Wolfgang Puck's famous pizza at Spago. LaDou also created the groundbreaking menu of California Pizza Kitchen. This particular pizza is full of flavor and textures, featuring sausage, eggplant, three kinds of cheese, olives, and roasted garlic for a mellow burst in each bite.

MAKES 1 (14-INCH) PIZZA, SERVES 2 TO 4

Make the pizza dough at least 24 hours ahead. Rest the dough on the counter until it comes to room temperature, about 1 hour. Make the roasted garlic cloves.

Move an oven rack to the lowest position. Preheat the oven to 500°F for 30 minutes.

Place the sausages in a small pan and bake for 10 minutes. Let cool for 5 minutes and then slice into thin rounds.

Toss the eggplant cubes and lemon zest in a bowl. Heat 2 tablespoons of the olive oil in a medium skillet over medium-high heat. Add the eggplant and stir with a wooden spoon until browned, about 10 minutes. Add the lemon juice and wine to the eggplant. Reduce the heat to low and simmer until the wine evaporates, about 5 minutes. Remove from the heat and let cool.

Shape the dough and place it on the screen, according to the instructions on page 40. Sprinkle with the Romano and then the mozzarella, leaving a 1-inch border. Top with the eggplant and the sausage rounds. Sprinkle with the feta, olives, roasted garlic cloves, and oregano. Drizzle the remaining olive oil over the toppings.

Bake the pizza for about 15 minutes, until the crust is deep brown and the toppings are bubbling. Check underneath with a metal spatula to ensure the bottom crust is deep brown too. Let the pizza rest for 5 minutes. Sprinkle with the parsley, cut into 8 wedges, and serve.

AHI TUNA PIZZA

Seared Tuna ▲ Tomato Sauce ▲ Capers

Naples-Style Pizza Dough (page 39)

FOR THE MARINATED TUNA

- 2 cloves garlic, chopped
- 1 tablespoon extra-virgin olive oil, plus more for serving
- 1/2 teaspoon dried oregano
- 1 (8-ounce) piece ahi tuna loin

Chunky Tomato Sauce (page 27)

FOR THE TUNA RUB

- 1 teaspoon dried oregano
- 1 teaspoon paprika
- 1/2 teaspoon salt
- 2 tablespoons extra-virgin olive oil
- 1/2 teaspoon freshly ground black pepper
- 1 ounce grated Parmigiano Reggiano (1/4 cup)
- 8 ounces fresh mozzarella, thinly sliced
- 1/2 cup thinly sliced white onion
- 2 tablespoons capers, preferably large
- 1/2 lemon
- 1 tablespoon chopped fresh flat-leaf parsley

With more than one hundred locations, both in Italy and worldwide, Fratelli la Bufala makes a world-class Neapolitan pizza. This pizza uses fresh cow's-milk mozzarella that produces a rich milky flavor. It pairs well with plump ripe tomatoes. You can use the softer, richer buffalo mozzarella, but it is difficult to find and can be expensive.

MAKES 1 (14-INCH) PIZZA, SERVES 3 TO 4

Make the pizza dough at least 24 hours ahead.

Make the Marinated Tuna: Place the garlic, oil, and oregano in a reclosable plastic bag. Seal and shake to cover. Marinate in the refrigerator for at least 12 hours or overnight.

Rest the dough on the counter until it comes to room temperature, about 1 hour. Make the chunky tomato sauce.

Move an oven rack to the lowest position. Preheat the oven to 500°F for 30 minutes.

Make the Tuna Rub: Mix all the ingredients in a small bowl. Remove the tuna from the marinade. Coat the tuna steak with the rub.

Heat a little olive oil in a small skillet over high heat and sear the tuna quickly, just a minute on

(continued)

each side. The tuna should be rare inside. Let it cool.

Shape the dough and place it on the pizza pan or screen, according to the instructions on page 40. Sprinkle with the Parmigiano Reggiano, leaving a 1-inch border. Spread the tomato sauce over the dough with a rubber spatula. Top with the mozzarella slices, followed by the onion slices and the capers.

Bake the pizza for 15 to 18 minutes, until the crust is deep brown and the toppings are bubbling. Check underneath with a metal spatula to ensure the bottom crust is deep brown too. Cut the tuna into 1/2-inch-thick slices and toss them on the pizza. Let the pizza rest for 5 minutes. Squeeze the lemon over the toppings, then sprinkle with the parsley. Cut it into 8 wedges and serve.

Sourcing Sustainable Tuna

Many tunas, particularly bluefin and big-eye, are overfished and caught in ways that endanger dolphins and sea turtles. Look for pole-caught yellowfin tuna instead. It's more sustainable because this kind of fishing doesn't kill other species, and it may contain less mercury because it's a smaller fish and harvested at a younger age. Go to Seafood Watch (www.seafoodwatch.org), a website that helps you select fish that are fished or farmed in ways that have less impact on the environment.

Cooked tuna is almost always served rare and seared around the edges. The texture is rich and smooth and tastes faintly like the ocean. Tuna actually tastes fishier when cooked through.

APIZZA AMORE

Tomato Sauce ▲ *Mozzarella* ▲ *Capicola*

Naples-Style Pizza
Dough (page 39)

Chunky Tomato Sauce
(page 27)

1 ounce grated
Parmigiano
Reggiano (¹/₄ cup)

4 ounces fresh
mozzarella, thinly
sliced

¹/₄ pound thinly sliced
capicola

Apizza Scholls takes its name from Scholls, Oregon, where the pizzeria began in a wood-fired sourdough bakery. Eventually the owners moved to Portland and their pizzeria became popular enough to attract the attention of *Food & Wine* magazine, which appointed Apizza Scholls pizzeria as one of the best in the country.

Make a classic Neapolitan pizza by skipping the meat and adding seven leaves of fresh basil once it comes out of the oven.

MAKES 1 (14-INCH) PIZZA, SERVES 2

Make the pizza dough at least 24 hours ahead. Rest the dough on the counter until it comes to room temperature, about I hour. Make the chunky tomato sauce.

Move an oven rack to the lowest position. Preheat the oven to 500°F for 30 minutes.

Shape the dough and place it on the screen, according to the instructions on page 40. Sprinkle with the Parmigiano Reggiano, leaving a I-inch border. Spread the tomato sauce over the dough with a rubber spatula. Top with the sliced mozzarella. Ball up the capicola slices and push them into the sauce.

Bake the pizza for about 15 minutes, until the crust is deep brown and the toppings are bubbling. Check underneath with a metal spatula to ensure the bottom crust is deep brown too. Let the pizza rest for 5 minutes. Cut it into 8 wedges and serve.

WHITE CLAM PIE

Clams ▲ Pecorino Romano ▲ Oregano

Naples-Style Pizza
Dough (page 39)

36 littleneck clams

1/2 cup grated Pecorino
Romano

1 tablespoon dried
oregano

1 teaspoon freshly
ground black
pepper

2 cloves garlic,
minced

1/4 cup extra-virgin
olive oil

FRANK PEPE
PIZZERIA NAPOLETANA,
NEW HAVEN, CONNECTICUT

Frank Pepe founded this pizzeria in 1925.
He served only two pies back then: one with
Romano, oregano, and tomatoes; and one with
anchovies and mozzarella. Frank got his inspi-
ration for the clam pie from the freshly shucked
clams he served in the bar. It was only a matter
of time before the clams found their way onto
the pizza.

This is a plain pie with lots of taste. It is
made without mozzarella because they say the
cheese overwhelms the clams and makes the pie
too rich. I think they are right—this is one of the
best pizzas I have ever had without mozzarella.

Littlenecks are one of the smallest clams.
They come 7 to 10 to a pound. Because they are
tiny, they cook quickly, and they are one of the
most tender clams to eat.

MAKES 1 (14-INCH) PIZZA, SERVES 2

Make the pizza dough at least 24 hours ahead.
Rest the dough on the counter until it comes to
room temperature, about 1 hour.

Move an oven rack to the lowest position.
Preheat the oven to 500°F for 30 minutes.

Bring 4 cups water to a boil in a large pot over
high heat. Place the clams in the boiling water
for about 1 minute. The clams will begin to open.
Transfer the open clams to a colander and run
cold water over them to cool them quickly. Slide
a knife in the crack and open them. Any clams
that do not open wide enough to slide a knife
into should be discarded. Put the clam meat on
paper towels and discard the shells. Pat the clam
meat dry.

Shape the dough and place it on the pizza pan
or screen, according to the instructions on
page 40. Place the clams on the pizza crust,
leaving a 1-inch border. Sprinkle with the Romano,
oregano, pepper, and garlic. Drizzle the olive oil
over the toppings.

Bake the pizza for about 15 minutes, until the
crust is deep brown and the toppings are bubbling. Check underneath with a metal spatula to
ensure the bottom crust is deep brown too. Let
the pizza rest for 5 minutes. Cut it into 8 wedges
and serve.

ARAGOSTA PIZZA

Lobster ▲ Garlic Butter ▲ Ricotta

Naples-Style Pizza Dough (page 39)

1 cup ricotta, preferably whole milk

2 lobster tails (about 6 ounces each)

5 tablespoons butter

3 cloves garlic, coarsely chopped

1/4 cup dry white wine, such as Pinot Grigio

1 tablespoon chopped fresh basil leaves, plus 7 leaves for garnish

1/2 teaspoon salt

1 ounce grated Parmigiano Reggiano (1/4 cup)

Lobster is synonymous with Maine, so it makes sense that Maine restaurants put the crustacean into just about every meal. Lobster is excellent on pizza, and it is worth every bite. The lobster is cooked the traditional way with butter, white wine, and garlic, and then placed on a bed of thickened ricotta to soak up its garlicky, buttery goodness.

MAKES 1 (14-INCH) PIZZA, SERVES 4

Make the pizza dough at least 24 hours ahead. Place the ricotta in a mesh strainer set in a bowl, and let it rest overnight in the refrigerator to drain. If the lobster tails are frozen, thaw them overnight in the fridge.

Rest the pizza dough on the counter until it comes to room temperature, about 1 hour.

Move an oven rack to the lowest position. Preheat the oven to 500°F for 30 minutes.

Cut the lobster shells down the middle on both sides, using scissors. Remove the meat from the shell. Lift out the black vein in the middle and discard. Chop the lobster meat into 1-inch chunks. Wash your hands after handling.

Heat 2 tablespoons of the butter and the garlic in a medium skillet over medium-low heat. Sauté the garlic for 30 seconds. Do not let it burn. Add the lobster and toss with the garlic butter, just long enough to coat it. Remove the lobster. Pour

In the white wine and let it reduce almost completely, about 5 minutes. Add the remaining 3 tablespoons butter and the chopped basil, salt, and Parmigiano Reggiano. Stir and cook for 1 minute more, until the sauce thickens. Remove from the heat.

Shape the dough and place it on the pizza pan or screen, according to the instructions on page 40. Use a rubber spatula to spread the drained ricotta evenly over the dough, leaving a 1-inch border. Spread the garlic butter sauce over the ricotta and scatter the lobster on top.

Bake the pizza for about 15 minutes, until the crust is deep brown and the toppings are bubbling. Check underneath with a metal spatula to ensure the bottom crust is deep brown too. Tear up the 7 basil leaves and toss them on top of the cooked pizza. Let the pizza rest for 5 minutes. Cut it into 8 wedges and serve.

WHITE BEAN PUREE PIE WITH ASPARAGUS

White Beans ▲ Rosemary ▲ Asparagus

Naples-Style Pizza Dough (page 39)

FOR THE GARLIC WHITE BEAN PUREE

1   (15-ounce) can white beans, such as cannellini or Great Northern, drained and rinsed

2   large cloves garlic, coarsely chopped

1   teaspoon chopped fresh rosemary leaves

1/2 teaspoon salt

1   teaspoon balsamic vinegar

2   tablespoons extra-virgin olive oil

Freshly ground black pepper

16 asparagus spears, trimmed

2   tablespoons extra-virgin olive oil

1/2 teaspoon dried thyme

1   ounce grated Parmigiano Reggiano (1/4 cup)

8   ounces fresh mozzarella

1   tablespoon chopped fresh flat-leaf parsley

Serious Pie has an authentic West Coast foodie vibe. It's a small neighborhood place, and everyone is friendly, happy, and easygoing. This pie layers on the flavors, starting with olive oil and thyme over the crust, a spread of garlicky white beans, spears of asparagus, and a topping of fresh mozzarella.

MAKES 1 (14-INCH) PIZZA, SERVES 2 TO 3

Make the pizza dough at least 24 hours ahead. Rest the dough on the counter until it comes to room temperature, about 1 hour.

Move an oven rack to the lowest position. Preheat the oven to 500°F for 30 minutes.

Make the White Bean Puree: Place the beans, garlic, rosemary, salt, vinegar, and olive oil in a food processor fitted with the metal blade and puree until smooth. Season to taste with pepper.

Bring a large pot of water to a boil. Add the asparagus and cook for 2 minutes, until crisp-tender. Transfer the spears to a colander and rinse with cold running water to cool.

Shape the dough and place it on the pizza pan or screen, according to the instructions on page 40. Mix the olive oil with the dried thyme in a small bowl. Brush the dough with half the thyme oil, leaving a 1-inch border. Sprinkle with the Parmigiano Reggiano. Drop spoonfuls of the bean puree on top. Place the asparagus in a spoke pattern on top of the puree. Tear the mozzarella into small pieces and scatter them over the pizza. Drizzle the remaining thyme oil over the pizza.

Bake the pizza for about 15 minutes, until the crust is deep brown and the toppings are bubbling. Check underneath with a metal spatula to ensure the bottom crust is deep brown too. Let the pizza rest for 5 minutes. Sprinkle with the parsley, then cut the pizza into 8 wedges and serve.

BAKED EGG AND EGGPLANT PIZZA

Eggs ▲ Roasted Eggplant ▲ Tomato Sauce

Naples-Style Pizza Dough (page 39)

Chunky Tomato Sauce (page 27)

1 medium eggplant (about 1.5 pounds), cut in 1-inch cubes

2 teaspoons salt

1/4 cup extra-virgin olive oil

2 ounces grated Parmigiano Reggiano (1/2 cup)

8 ounces fresh mozzarella, thinly sliced

3 large eggs

1 tablespoon chopped fresh flat-leaf parsley

Chef Marco Wiles showcases wine and hand-made rustic pizzas at this shabby-chic destination in Houston. Dolce Vita aims to re-create the taste of authentic Neapolitan pizza. This elegant pizza features creamy eggplant that pairs well with the richness of egg yolk. This may seem like an unusual combination, but it will knock you out.

MAKES 1 (14-INCH) PIZZA, SERVES 2 TO 3

Make the pizza dough at least 24 hours ahead. Rest the dough on the counter until it comes to room temperature, about 1 hour. Make the chunky tomato sauce.

Move an oven rack to the lowest position. Preheat the oven to 500°F for 30 minutes.

In a medium bowl, toss the eggplant cubes with the salt and let sit for about 20 minutes. A little water will seep from the eggplant, making the eggplant creamy and soft when cooked. Transfer the eggplant to a colander to drain, and rinse well with cold running water.

Heat the olive oil in a medium skillet over medium heat. Add the eggplant and sauté for about 15 minutes, stirring often so the eggplant cooks evenly. It will be soft and dark brown when ready.

Shape the dough and place it on the pizza pan or screen, according to the instructions on page 40. Sprinkle with 1/4 cup of the Parmesan, leaving a 1-inch border. Spread the tomato sauce over the dough and Parmigiano Reggiano with a rubber spatula. Top with the mozzarella slices, then the eggplant.

Bake the pizza for 12 minutes. Open the oven door flat and pull out the rack partway. Sprinkle the remaining 1/4 cup Parmigiano Reggiano over the pizza. Carefully crack the eggs over the center of the pizza. Bake for about 6 minutes more. Remove the pizza when the eggs are still soft. The crust should be deep brown and the sauce should be bubbling. Check underneath with a metal spatula to ensure the bottom crust is deep brown too. Let the pizza rest for 5 minutes. Sprinkle with the parsley, then cut the pizza into 8 wedges and serve.

CAULIFLOWER ASADO PIZZA

Roasted Cauliflower ▲ Lime Verde Sauce ▲ Gruyère

PIZZERIA SEVEN TWELVE, OREM, UTAH

Naples-Style Pizza Dough (page 39)

FOR THE ROASTED CAULIFLOWER

1 small head cauliflower

2 tablespoons butter, melted

1 tablespoon chopped fresh rosemary

1 teaspoon salt

FOR THE LIME VERDE SAUCE

1 tablespoon extra-virgin olive oil

1/4 cup chopped white onion

1 jalapeño pepper, seeded

1 clove garlic, coarsely chopped

2 (4.5-ounce) cans roasted green chiles

Zest and juice of 1 lime

1 teaspoon all-purpose flour

1/4 cup white vinegar

1 teaspoon salt

1 teaspoon freshly ground black pepper

1 teaspoon sugar

1/4 cup chopped fresh cilantro (from about 1/4 bunch)

1 tablespoon butter

1 medium yellow onion, peeled and thinly sliced

3 ounces Gruyère, shredded (1 cup)

The folks at Pizzeria Seven Twelve share the bounty of good simple food and all that it encompasses. That includes the community, where farmers know the chefs by name. Their familiarity is more than a trend—it's a way to live and to eat. This pizza has a familiar taste because of the roasted cauliflower and sautéed onions, but with the tang of green chiles, which makes a unique base sauce.

MAKES 1 (14-INCH) PIZZA, SERVES 2 TO 3

Make the pizza dough at least 24 hours ahead. Rest the dough on the counter until it comes to room temperature, about 1 hour.

Preheat the oven to 375°F.

Make the Roasted Cauliflower: Cut the cauliflower into 1-inch florets and discard the core. Toss the florets on a half sheet pan with the butter, rosemary, and salt. Roast for 30 minutes until browned.

Increase the oven temperature to 500°F and heat for 15 minutes. Move a rack to the lowest position.

Make the Lime Verde Sauce: Heat the olive oil in a small saucepan over high heat. Add the onion, jalapeño, garlic, and 1 can of chiles and cook, stirring often, for 1 minute. Add the lime zest and flour and stir well. Add the lime juice to the pot. Add 1/2 cup water and the vinegar. Reduce the heat to low and simmer until there is almost no more liquid, about 5 minutes. Stir often to prevent sticking, particularly toward the end. Add the salt, pepper, and sugar. Pour the sauce into a small bowl. Add the remaining can of chiles and the chopped cilantro and stir to combine.

Heat the butter in a small skillet over medium-low heat. Add the onion and sauté, stirring occasionally, until golden brown, about 15 minutes.

Shape the dough and place it on the pizza pan or screen, according to the instructions on page 40. Spread the salsa verde on the dough with a rubber spatula, leaving a 1-inch border. Sprinkle with the Gruyère, followed by the onion, and then the cauliflower.

Bake the pizza for 15 to 20 minutes, until the crust is deep brown and the toppings are bubbling. Check underneath with a metal spatula to ensure the bottom crust is deep brown too. Let the pizza rest for 5 minutes, then cut it into 8 wedges, and serve.

The Versatile Salsa Verde

Many Latin green sauces are made with fresh herbs like cilantro, plus tomatillos or raw green tomatoes. The Argentinean version, chimichurri, is made with parsley, vinegar, and garlic, and the French *sauce verte* includes basil and Dijon mustard. There are German and Italian green versions as well.

This sauce is Mexican, a blend of roasted chile peppers and herbs, with lime to brighten. If you enjoy it, whip up a batch as a dip for chicken wings or tortilla chips, or as a marinade and basting sauce for grilled pork. Thin it with a little oil or butter. Serve it with fish too, as a chunky relish on the side.

PESTO PIZZA

Pesto ▲ *Roasted Tomatoes* ▲ *Pine Nuts*

Naples-Style Pizza
  Dough (page 39)

Pesto Sauce (page 30)

Roasted Tomatoes
  (page 31)

2 tablespoons grated
   Parmigiano
   Reggiano

8 ounces fresh
   mozzarella, cut into
   1/4-inch-thick slices

2 tablespoons pine
   nuts

The Parlor has its own kitchen garden where chefs pick the fresh produce that appears on their pizzas. But growing your own tomatoes only gets you so far. The pizzas here excel because of the chefs' dedication to culinary excellence and their skill with the dough. Here's a simple earthy pesto pizza, with roasted tomato to elevate it a notch by adding bright acidity and sweetness.

MAKES 1 (14-INCH) PIZZA, SERVES 2 TO 3

Make the pizza dough at least 24 hours ahead. Rest the dough on the counter until it comes to room temperature, about 1 hour.

Make the pesto sauce and the roasted tomatoes. Move an oven rack to the lowest position and increase the oven temperature to 500°F. Heat for 15 minutes.

Shape the dough and place it on the pizza pan or screen, according to the instructions on page 40. Sprinkle with the Parmigiano Reggiano. Spread the pesto over the dough with a rubber spatula, leaving a 1-inch border. Make a single layer of the mozzarella slices, then top with the roasted tomatoes.

Place the pine nuts in a dry skillet over medium-high heat and toss until browned, about 3 minutes.

Bake the pizza for about 15 minutes, until the crust is deep brown and the toppings are bubbling. Check underneath with a metal spatula to ensure the bottom crust is deep brown too. Let the pizza rest for 5 minutes. Sprinkle with the toasted pine nuts, then cut the pizza into 8 wedges and serve.

SUMMER SQUASH PIZZA

Roasted Zucchini ▲ *Truffle Oil* ▲ *Truffled Cheese*

Naples-Style Pizza Dough (page 39)

Roasted Zucchini (page 34)

1 ounce grated Parmigiano Reggiano (1/4 cup)

1 tablespoon white truffle oil

4 ounces Sottocenere

1 tablespoon chopped fresh flat-leaf parsley

Osteria is driven by the passions of James Beard Award–winning chef Jeff Michaud. Its menu changes seasonally, so this beautiful summer squash pizza may not appear at other times of the year. Make this truffled pizza to enjoy a glimpse of Osteria's genius. He uses Sottocenere, a semi-hard to hard Italian cheese with black truffles. If you can't find it, substitute Edam and drizzle truffle oil over the cooked pizza.

MAKES 1 (14-INCH) PIZZA, SERVES 2 TO 3

Make the pizza dough at least 24 hours ahead. Rest the dough on the counter until it comes to room temperature, about I hour.

Make the roasted zucchini. Move an oven rack to the lowest position and increase the oven temperature to 500°F. Heat for I5 minutes.

Shape the dough and place it on the pizza pan or screen, according to the instructions on page 40. Sprinkle with the Parmigiano Reggiano, leaving a I-inch border, and drizzle with the truffle oil.

Crumble the Sottocenere with your fingers and sprinkle it over the top. Overlap the zucchini slices around the pizza to form concentric circles.

Bake the pizza for about I5 minutes, until the crust is deep brown and the toppings are bubbling. Check underneath with a metal spatula to ensure the bottom crust is deep brown too. Let the pizza rest for 5 minutes. Sprinkle with the parsley, then cut the pizza into 8 wedges and serve.

PEPE PIZZA

Creamed Leeks ▲ Bell Peppers ▲ Basil

Naples-Style Pizza
   Dough (page 39)
1   large leek
2   tablespoons butter
5   fresh basil leaves,
    chopped
1   cup heavy cream
5   ounces Caciotta,
    grated (2 cups)

1   teaspoon salt
1   red bell pepper,
    seeded and halved
1   orange or green bell
    pepper, seeded and
    halved
1   teaspoon extra-
    virgin olive oil

Flour + Water has an advantage over most other restaurants because of its local community of artisan purveyors. The restaurant's mantra of "refurbish, repurpose, and reclaim" is the way chef Thomas McNaughton sees its mission. Building the restaurant with reused materials helped it fit right into a community of artists, environmentalists, and activists. So did having killer Italian cuisine. Handmade pasta and pizzas are the specialty.

This is a rich pizza with a creamy leek and Caciotta cheese. There are many kinds of Caciotta, a simple Tuscan cheese with a soft yellow rind. You want one that is semi-firm. It also comes with ancho chiles, peppercorns, and truffles, so if you would like a flavored cheese, it will add another note to your pizza. If you can't find Caciotta, substitute Edam or Gouda.

MAKES 1 (14-INCH) PIZZA, SERVES 2 TO 3

Make the pizza dough at least 24 hours ahead. Rest the dough on the counter until it comes to room temperature, about 1 hour.

Preheat the oven to 350°F.

Remove the outer leaves of the leek if they are wilted. Cut the leek into 4 sections about 3 inches long. Remove the tough outer green leaves around each section. Cut the leeks in half lengthwise and then slice the halves into thin strips. Place the strips in a colander and wash with cold running water to remove all dirt.

Melt the butter in a medium skillet over medium-low heat. Add about half the leek strips. Sauté until limp, about 10 minutes. Add the basil leaves and cream to the skillet. Increase the heat to medium and reduce until thick and creamy, stirring occasionally, about 10 minutes. Add 1 cup of the grated cheese and the salt, and stir until blended. Turn off the heat.

Place the remaining leek strips on a dry sheet pan and bake for 15 minutes. The leek will be charred and crispy. Transfer the strips to a small bowl.

Turn the oven to broil. Place the red and orange bell pepper halves on a sheet pan, cut-side down, and brush the tops with the olive oil. Broil until the skins char, about 10 minutes. Set aside the

peppers until cool enough to handle, about 5 minutes, and then remove their skins. Cut the peppers into 1-inch squares.

Move an oven rack to the lowest position and increase the oven temperature to 500°F. Heat for 15 minutes.

Shape the dough and place it on the pizza pan or screen, according to the instructions on page 40. Spread the creamy leek sauce on top with a rubber spatula, leaving a 1-inch border. Sprinkle with the remaining cup of Caciotta. Top with the roasted pepper squares.

Bake the pizza for 15 to 20 minutes, until the crust is deep brown and the toppings are bubbling. Check underneath with a metal spatula to ensure the bottom crust is deep brown too. Immediately after removing the pizza from the oven, pile stacks of the charred leek in the center for a dramatic presentation. Let the pizza rest for 5 minutes. Cut it into 8 wedges and serve.

Chapter 4

NEW YORK-STYLE PIZZAS

Pizza did not exist in America until 1897, when an immigrant from Naples opened an Italian grocery store in Manhattan's Little Italy. Even then, most pizza was peddled on the street. In 1905, Gennaro Lombardi opened Lombardi's, the first pizzeria in America, and the first real pizzeria in New York City.

The pizza style was from Naples, but it had changed. The 00 flour Neapolitan pizzaiolos used was not available here, so unbleached flours of high protein took the place of the softer flour. This enabled the pizzaiolos to make larger, thinner pizzas stretched to 36 inches or more, coaxing the dough into a large round with their hands. Then they tossed it into the air with a spin, so centrifugal force created a larger circle with a weightier rim.

As in Italy, they sold their pizzas in slices. A slice of New York pie was large and flexible, with a foldable crust and a good chew. The bottom could be lightly charred from a coal oven burning at over 800°F. Traditionally these pies had a light tomato sauce with perhaps a sprinkle of mozzarella. Toppings were confined to one or two varieties, if used at all.

The popularity of New York–style pizza grew quickly across the United States. Pizza makers embraced the techniques and ingredients, and hand-tossed dough became the base for countless pizzas. Because the sturdy New York crust can hold a variety of toppings and sauces, it is now the go-to dough for most pizzerias.

Tradition has taken a back seat to ingenuity—New York pizzas get more imaginative all the time. The tastes of the nation's favorite snacks such as Buffalo wings and jalapeño poppers work their way onto a New York crust. Pizza melds with tacos in Hays, Kansas. The famous Hot Brown sandwich that originated in Louisville, Kentucky, turns into a pizza with roast turkey and cheesy Mornay sauce.

NEW YORK-STYLE PIZZA DOUGH

1³/₄ cups bread flour, plus more for dusting

2 teaspoons sugar

1 teaspoon active dry yeast

¹/₂ cup plus 3 tablespoons water

1 tablespoon extra-virgin olive oil, plus more for greasing

¹/₂ teaspoon salt

This dough makes a crispy crust with a chewy rim, the kind you'll see at good pizzerias all over New York. Letting the dough rise overnight lets the yeast do a better job at fermentation over a longer time, building flavor and texture.

Some recipes call for a hand-tossed dough, so I have included the instructions to do so. It's fun! It's not about throwing a pizza in the air, but about a way to stretch it quickly.

This recipe gets your dough onto a pan, ready for the toppings.

MAKES DOUGH FOR 1 (16-INCH) PIZZA CRUST

Place the flour, sugar, and yeast in the bowl of a stand mixer fitted with the dough hook. Mix on low to combine, about 5 seconds. Add the water and the olive oil and mix until a ball forms, about 2 minutes.

Turn off the mixer and let the dough rest for about 10 minutes. Add the salt. Knead on medium speed for 12 minutes. If the dough is too wet or sticky, add a teaspoon of flour and mix until a ball comes cleanly off the side of the bowl. When the dough is ready it should be firm, smooth, and supple.

To test elasticity, hold a 1-inch piece between your fingers and stretch the dough to make a windowpane. It should look like bubblegum (see page 20). If not, knead for 5 minutes more and test again. Keep going until the dough passes the test, up to 30 minutes more.

Pour a teaspoon of olive oil into a medium bowl. Wet your hands with water, shape the dough into a ball, and place it in the bowl. Turn the dough to coat it with oil. This prevents a crust from forming on its surface as it rises. Cover the bowl with plastic wrap and let the dough rise in the refrigerator overnight or up to 72 hours. After about 12 hours, the dough will be wider and taller, approximately doubled in size. Rest the dough on the counter until it comes to room temperature, about 1 hour.

(continued)

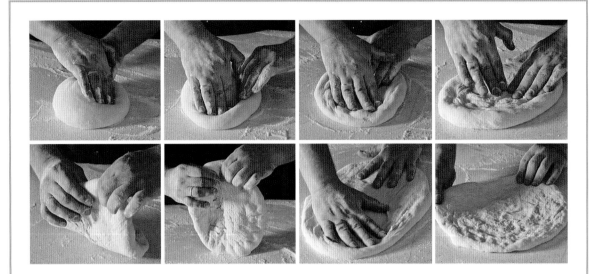

Get the Dough in Shape

STRETCH THE DOUGH Lightly flour a clean, dry countertop. Gently place the round of dough on your counter. Do not knead or press on it. Instead, let it settle. Dust the top with flour.

Make dimples in the dough with your fingertips by pressing down in the middle to stretch it out. At the same time, move the dough around in a circle with your fingertips. A 1-inch rim should form naturally. Press your fingertips along the inside of the rim, moving in a circle. Place your hands on the dough, fingers up against the rim, and push out while turning in a circle. Add more flour if necessary, to ensure the dough slides easily.

Pick up the dough to finish stretching it out. Slide your hands underneath and pick it up. Let the dough fall around your hands to stretch it. Keep your hands along the edges, rather than in the middle. The dough should be 16 inches in diameter.

HAND-TOSSING TECHNIQUE The New York dough is a good one to hand-toss because it's sturdy, flexible, and stretches well, and it's not sticky. You can hand-toss any of the pizza doughs in this chapter if you like.

Pick up the dough and, with your palms down, drape the dough over the knuckles of both hands. Toss the dough a few inches into the air and put a little spin on it to rotate the dough. Do this several times and keep the dough close to your hands. Don't throw it up into the air. That is not necessary and it will probably end up on the floor. The dough should be thin in the center with a ring around the edge. It should be about 16 inches in diameter.

PLACE THE DOUGH ON THE PAN OR SCREEN Spray a round 16-inch pizza pan with nonstick cooking spray and then lightly coat with flour. Place the pan next to the dough on the counter and quickly pick up the crust while sliding it onto the pan. Reshape as necessary into a round or oval shape. Your New York–style dough is now ready for the pizza toppings.

PROSCIUTTO PIZZA

Pesto ▲ *Prosciutto* ▲ *Ricotta*

New York–Style Pizza
Dough (page 63)

New York–Style Pizza
Sauce (page 28)

Pesto Sauce (page 30)

1   cup shredded
    mozzarella

1   cup ricotta

4   ounces thinly sliced
    prosciutto

**HUMBLE CRUMB,
GEORGETOWN,
SOUTH CAROLINA**

A sophisticated Southern town, Georgetown was the first landing place of European settlers in America. Perhaps those settlers brought the pizza bug when they landed, because even though Southern cooking is the leading cuisine here, pizza is a close second.

Humble Crumb is one of the reasons pizza is so popular here. At this family-owned restaurant, pizzas are made simply, from scratch, with the motto "Our food will leave you feeling good and satisfied." What could be simpler than that?

Here is one of the restaurant's Italian-inspired pizzas with pesto and prosciutto. These are honest and familiar flavors, prepared well.

MAKES 1 (16-INCH) PIZZA, SERVES 2 TO 3

Make the pizza dough at least 12 hours ahead. Rest the dough on the counter until it comes to room temperature, about 1 hour. Make the pizza sauce at least 1 hour ahead. Make the pesto sauce.

Move an oven rack to the lowest position. Preheat the oven to 500°F for 30 minutes.

Shape the dough and place it on the pizza pan or screen, according to the instructions on page 64. Spread the pizza sauce on the dough with a rubber spatula, leaving a 1-inch rim around the edge. Sprinkle with the mozzarella. Drop spoonfuls of ricotta over the pizza, leaving an inch between them. Place spoonfuls of pesto between the dollops of ricotta. Ball up the proscuitto slices and place them on the pizza. You should have a colorful pattern of red, green, white, and brown on top.

Bake the pizza for 15 to 20 minutes, until the crust is deep brown and the toppings are bubbling. Check underneath with a metal spatula to ensure the bottom crust is deep brown too. Let the pizza rest for 5 minutes. Cut it into 8 wedges and serve.

TACO PIZZA

Refried Beans ▲ Spicy Ground Beef ▲ Salsa

New York–Style Pizza Dough (page 63)

1 tablespoon extra-virgin olive oil

1/4 cup diced onion

1 clove garlic, chopped

1 (15-ounce) can pinto beans, drained and rinsed

1/2 teaspoon salt

1/4 teaspoon freshly ground pepper

12 ounces ground beef

1 (1.25-ounce) packet taco seasoning mix

1 cup shredded mozzarella

1 cup shredded cheddar

1 cup chunky salsa, such as Pace

2 cups shredded iceberg lettuce

1/2 cup diced tomato

Wild Bill Hickok was the sheriff in this town for a time in the 1800s. Buffalo Bill ran the railroad, and George Custer and Calamity Jane were notable residents. By 1872, many of the rougher elements had left for more action in nearby Dodge City (as in "get out of Dodge"), and Hays was left to become the county seat.

Today, Hays is a major university town with over eleven thousand students eating—what else?—pizza. Kids love tacos too, so Lomato's pizza got both of these major food groups into one pie. The result is an irresistible combination for college students that you can enjoy as well. The pizza incorporates refried beans, spicy ground meat, shredded cheddar, and tomato salsa. You've got all the components of a great taco, built on a New York crust.

MAKES 1 (16-INCH) PIZZA, SERVES 2 TO 3

Make the pizza dough at least 12 hours ahead. Rest the dough on the counter until it comes to room temperature, about 1 hour.

Move an oven rack to the lowest position. Preheat the oven to 500°F for 30 minutes.

Heat a medium skillet over medium heat. Add the olive oil and sauté the onion and garlic until soft, about 3 minutes. Add the pinto beans and sauté for 2 minutes more. Add 1/2 cup water and let the beans simmer, stirring occasionally, until the liquid evaporates, about 8 minutes. Add the salt and pepper and stir. Transfer the beans to a medium bowl and mash them with a fork.

Wipe out the skillet with a paper towel. Brown the beef in the same pan over medium-high heat, breaking it up with a spoon, about 4 minutes. Add the taco seasoning and 3/4 cup water and reduce to a simmer. Cook, stirring occasionally, until the water evaporates, about 5 minutes.

Shape the dough and place it on the screen, according to the instructions on page 64. Spread the beans on the dough with a rubber spatula, all the way to the edges. Sprinkle with the mozzarella and cheddar. Drop spoonfuls of the taco meat and salsa on top.

Bake the pizza for about 15 minutes, until the crust is deep brown and the toppings are bubbling. Check underneath with a metal spatula to ensure the bottom crust is deep brown too. Let the pizza rest for 5 minutes. Top with the shredded lettuce and chopped tomato. Cut the pizza into 8 wedges and serve.

SOPLA FUEGO

Habanero Sauce ▲ Chorizo ▲ Avocado

New York–Style Pizza Dough (page 63)

FOR THE HABANERO PIZZA SAUCE

- 1 tablespoon extra-virgin olive oil
- 1/3 cup minced peeled carrot
- 2 tablespoons chopped onion
- 1/2 to 1 whole fresh habanero chile, seeded
- 1 clove garlic, minced
- 1/2 cup chopped mango or papaya
- 1/2 cup diced tomatoes, preferably canned
- 1/3 cup apple cider
- 1 tablespoon sugar
- 1 teaspoon red wine vinegar
- 1/2 teaspoon salt

- 1 (16-ounce) package fresh chorizo, casings removed
- 1 cup shredded mozzarella
- 1/2 cup thinly sliced red onion
- 1/2 cup thinly sliced red bell peppers
- 4 ounces fresh Mexican cheese (queso fresco), crumbled (about 1 cup)
- 1/2 cup sour cream
- 1 avocado, thinly sliced
- 1/4 cup chopped fresh cilantro (from about 1/4 bunch)

Detroit needs big, bold flavors to keep its residents warm on those cold winter nights. That's why Motor City Brewing Works is so popular. This pizza, with a habanero pepper sauce, is just spicy enough to get your motor running. Add chorizo, bell peppers, avocado, and sour cream and you'll head out on that highway with a huge grin.

MAKES 1 (16-INCH) PIZZA, SERVES 3 TO 4

Make the pizza dough at least 12 hours ahead. Rest the dough on the counter until it comes to room temperature, about 1 hour.

Move an oven rack to the lowest position. Preheat the oven to 500°F for 30 minutes.

Make the Habanero Pizza Sauce: Heat the olive oil in a medium saucepan over medium-high heat. Add the carrot, onion, chile, garlic, and mango and sauté for 1 minute. Add the tomatoes, apple cider,

sugar, vinegar, and salt and stir. Reduce the heat to medium. Simmer for about 10 minutes, stirring occasionally to prevent scorching, until the liquid evaporates. Let cool. The sauce should be thick. If not, simmer for a few minutes more until it is the consistency of pizza sauce.

Heat a large skillet over medium heat. Cook the chorizo, breaking it up with a spoon, until browned and crumbly, about 10 minutes. Use a slotted spoon to transfer the chorizo to a bowl lined with paper towels.

Shape the dough and place it on the pizza pan or screen, according to the instructions on page 64. Spread the habanero sauce over the dough with a rubber spatula, leaving a l-inch rim around the edge. Sprinkle with the mozzarella, cooked chorizo, and sliced onion and bell peppers. Scatter the cheese over the pizza.

Bake the pizza for l5 to 20 minutes, until the crust is deep brown and the toppings are bubbling. Check underneath with a metal spatula to ensure the bottom crust is deep brown too. Let the pizza rest for 5 minutes.

Meanwhile, spoon the sour cream into a small plastic bag. Squeeze it into one corner. Snip the corner to create a tiny hole and squeeze out the sour cream in a thin stream. Swirl it back and forth over the whole pizza. Top with the avocado slices and cilantro. Cut the pizza into 8 wedges and serve.

Habanero

HOW MUCH HEAT DO YOU LIKE?

The heat of these piquant habanero chiles lives in the seeds and membrane. If you want a fiery pizza, leave them in. Otherwise, enjoy its fruity and smoky flavor in a milder version of this pizza.

Related to the Scotch bonnet, and often used interchangeably, habaneros were once the hottest chiles of all. More recently, the Carolina Reaper was named the world's hottest pepper, dethroning the Ghost pepper from Bangladesh and Moruga Scorpion from Trinidad. Pepper heat is measured in Scoville Heat Units, and the Reaper has more than a million. The habanero, however, has a mere 300,000.

THE DELUXE

Mushrooms ▲ Sausage ▲ Bacon

New York–Style Pizza Dough (page 63), with variation below

Cooked Tomato Sauce (page 27)

Sautéed Mushrooms (page 34)

1   mild Italian sausage link (about 4 ounces)

5   ounces bacon (5 strips)

All-purpose flour, for dusting

Nonstick cooking spray

1   cup shredded mozzarella

2   ounces Provel, shredded (about 1 cup)

¹/₂   cup sliced green bell pepper

¹/₂   cup sliced white onion

IMO'S PIZZA, ST. LOUIS, MISSOURI

Ed and Marge Imo opened Imo's Pizza over forty years ago. Their pizza's unique style became known as St. Louis–style pizza. Characterized by a thin, crackerlike crust made without yeast, it is dressed edge-to-edge and cut into squares, perhaps because Ed Imo was a tile layer.

The St. Louis style requires a special cheese called Provel. Made from three cheeses fused to form one—provolone, Swiss, and white cheddar—Provel is not widely sold outside the St. Louis area, but can be substituted by combining Swiss, sharp cheddar, and smoked provolone in equal parts. The original is much better, though. You can order Provel online, and it is worth it. It has a creaminess that can't be beat or duplicated.

The Imo's crust is similar to New York pizza dough, but uses half the amount and substitutes baking powder for yeast. This creates a thin, dry, flaky crust no thicker than ¹/₈ inch thick. The dough is docked, with many tiny holes that allow steam to escape, so the crust stays flat and thin. Even though the crust is thin, this pizza can hold its many toppings, and the square cut keeps them anchored on top.

MAKES 1 (16-INCH) PIZZA, SERVES 2 TO 3

Make the New York pizza dough according to the first step in the dough recipe on page 63, but substitute ¹/₂ teaspoon baking powder for the yeast. Since there is no yeast in the dough, it doesn't need time to rise.

Divide the dough in half and form it into 2 dough balls. Oil each dough ball with a teaspoon of oil to keep them from creating a skin on the outside. Freeze one ball in a freezer bag for up to

3 months. Let the remaining dough ball rest for 30 minutes at room temperature before rolling it out.

Make the cooked tomato sauce at least 1 hour ahead. Make the sautéed mushrooms.

Preheat the oven to 400°F.

Place the sausages and bacon on a sheet pan and place in the oven. After 10 minutes, remove the sausages and drain on paper towels. Let cool for 5 minutes, then slice into rounds. Cook the bacon 5 minutes longer. Drain on paper towels.

Move an oven rack to the lowest position. Increase the temperature to 500°F and heat for 15 minutes.

Lightly flour a clean, dry countertop. Put the dough in the center and sprinkle a little flour on top. Roll out the dough, using a rolling pin, starting from the center out to the edges. Work around the dough to form a circular 16-inch shaped dough with even thickness. Then use a dough docker or a fork to prick the dough all over with tiny holes.

Cover a 16-inch pizza pan or screen with non-stick cooking spray and transfer the dough to it. Reshape as necessary.

Spread the sauce on the dough with a rubber spatula, all the way out to the edges. Sprinkle with the mozzarella and Provel. Distribute the sausage rounds, bacon strips, sautéed mushrooms, peppers, and onion evenly over the entire pizza.

Bake the pizza for about 15 minutes, until the crust is deep brown, the toppings are bubbling, and the bacon is crisp. Check underneath with a metal spatula to ensure the bottom crust is deep brown too. Let the pizza rest for 5 minutes. To be traditional, cut into 16 squares and serve.

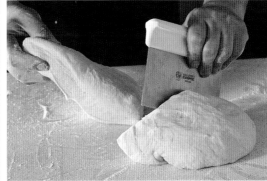

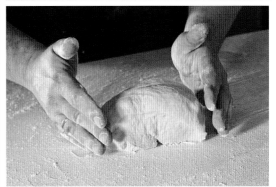

UFF DA PIZZA

Wild Rice ▲ Canadian Bacon ▲ Mushrooms

New York–Style Pizza Dough (page 63)

Chunky Tomato Sauce (page 27)

Sautéed Mushrooms (page 34)

2 ounces wild rice, cooked (1 cup)

1 ounce Parmigiano Reggiano, grated (¹/4 cup)

6 ounces fresh mozzarella

2 tablespoons extra-virgin olive oil

4 ounces Canadian bacon (4 slices), quartered

¹/2 cup coarsely chopped red onion

In the sleepy lake town of Grand Marais, tourists flock to pizza for its familiarity and comfort. Sven and Ole's Pizza reflects its Nordic roots in a casual and fun way, with illustrations of little Nordic dudes and a warm Velcome sign.

Sven and Ole's has come a long way since its humble beginnings. Two young men opened a nacho stand to sell snacks during the summer in 1981. The next season they stayed open all year and added pizza to their menu. Named for an all-purpose Norwegian exclamation, the Uff Da pizza features wild rice and Canadian bacon, typical Minnesota flavors. A zingy tomato sauce brings them together in this tasty, unusual pizza.

MAKES 1 (16-INCH) PIZZA, SERVES 3 TO 4

Make the pizza dough at least 12 hours ahead. Rest the dough on the counter until it comes to room temperature, about 1 hour. Make the chunky tomato sauce at least 1 hour ahead. Make the sautéed mushrooms.

Move an oven rack to the lowest position. Preheat the oven to 500°F for 30 minutes.

Shape the dough and place it on the pizza pan or screen, according to the instructions on page 64. Spread the tomato sauce over the dough with a rubber spatula, leaving a 1-inch rim around the edge. Distribute the wild rice on top. Sprinkle with the Parmigiano Reggiano. Tear the mozzarella into small pieces and scatter them over the pizza. Top with the Canadian bacon, onion, and sautéed mushroom.

Bake the pizza for 15 to 20 minutes, until the crust is deep brown and the toppings are bubbling. Check underneath with a metal spatula to ensure the bottom crust is deep brown too. Let the pizza rest for 5 minutes. Cut it into 8 wedges and serve.

MARGHERITA PIZZA

Tomato ▲ Basil ▲ Fresh Mozzarella

New York–Style Pizza Dough (page 63)

New York–Style Pizza Sauce (page 28)

8 ounces fresh mozzarella, thinly sliced

2 tablespoons grated Parmigiano Reggiano

1/2 teaspoon dried oregano

7 fresh basil leaves

Patsy's is the very definition of "old school." This New York pizza joint has been making thin coal-charred slices since 1933. The Margherita is the house specialty. Pasquale "Patsy" Lancieri made it with simple authentic flavors, served in the tradition of his homeland. Great pizza brings in great clientele. At Patsy's, luminaries like Frank Sinatra, Dean Martin, and Tony Bennett became regulars. Politicians past and present, including Spiro Agnew, Adam Clayton Powell, and New York City mayors, have used Pasty's as a place to communicate with the neighborhood. The place is as genuine as it gets. So is the pizza. It's big, usually 24 inches wide, which is a hard size to bake at home. I cut it down to a 16-inch pie. Try this for a classic old-world taste.

MAKES 1 (16-INCH) PIZZA, SERVES 2 TO 3

Make the pizza dough at least 12 hours ahead. Rest the dough on the counter until it comes to room temperature, about 1 hour. Make the pizza sauce at least 1 hour ahead.

Move an oven rack to the lowest position. Preheat the oven to 500°F for 30 minutes.

Shape the dough and place it on the pizza pan or screen, according to the instructions on page 64. Spread the pizza sauce on the dough with a rubber spatula, leaving a 1-inch rim around the edge. Cover with the mozzarella.

Bake the pizza for 15 minutes, until the crust is deep brown and the toppings are bubbling. Check underneath with a metal spatula to ensure the bottom crust is deep brown too. Let the pizza rest for 5 minutes. Sprinkle with the Parmigiano Reggiano and the dried oregano. Tear the basil leaves and scatter them over the top. Cut the pizza into 8 wedges and serve.

DARKWING DUCK PIZZA

Duck Proscuitto ▲ *Brussels Sprouts* ▲ *Balsamic Vinegar*

ROBERTA'S PIZZA, BROOKLYN, NEW YORK

New York–Style Pizza Dough (page 63)

Herbed Olive Oil (page 31)

FOR THE BALSAMIC SYRUP

1/2 cup good-quality balsamic vinegar

1/2 teaspoon honey

1 bay leaf

2 tablespoons unsalted butter

8 ounces brussels sprouts, coarsely chopped

2 tablespoons sugar

2 tablespoons apple cider vinegar

1 teaspoon salt

1/2 teaspoon crushed red pepper flakes

3 ounces Pecorino Romano, grated (1/4 cup)

8 ounces Chandoka, shredded (2 cups)

4 ounces duck breast prosciutto, thinly sliced

I had never come across a duck pizza until I found Roberta's. This pie features duck proscuitto, brussels sprouts, and Chandoka, a Wisconsin cheese made from goat's and cow's milk. It is similar to Edam or a goat's-milk Gouda. Order duck proscuitto online, or if you're feeling ambitious, cure your own. It tastes like duck bacon, and the fat melts into the brussels sprouts, giving them a rich, slightly salty edge. The balsamic syrup is my addition, just a little splash to add more tang. If you can't find Chandoka, substitute white cheddar, preferably made with goat's milk.

MAKES 1 (16-INCH) PIZZA, SERVES 3 TO 4

Make the pizza dough at least 12 hours ahead. Rest the dough on the counter until it comes to room temperature, about 1 hour. Make the herbed olive oil.

Move an oven rack to the lowest position. Preheat the oven to 500°F for 30 minutes.

Make the Balsamic Syrup: Put the vinegar, honey, and bay leaf in a heavy-bottomed small saucepan over medium-high heat. Bring to a simmer. Cook, stirring frequently until it is the consistency of thick maple syrup, 10 to 15 minutes. You should have about 2 tablespoons. Discard the bay leaf.

Melt the butter in a medium skillet over medium-high heat. Add the brussels sprouts, sugar, vinegar, salt, and red pepper flakes and toss well with tongs. Reduce the heat to medium and cook for

about 10 minutes, until limp, stirring occasionally. Drain in a colander set in the sink.

Shape the dough and place it on the pizza pan or screen, according to the instructions on page 64. Spread the herbed oil over the dough with a pastry brush, covering the entire surface. Sprinkle with the Romano, leaving a 1-inch border, then top with the shredded Chandoka. Cover the cheese with the brussels sprouts, then add the proscuitto slices.

Bake the pizza for about 15 minutes, until the crust is deep brown and the toppings are bubbling. Check underneath with a metal spatula to ensure the bottom crust is deep brown too. Let the pizza rest for 5 minutes. Sprinkle with the balsamic syrup. Cut it into 8 wedges and serve.

BANSUECCIO PIZZA

Smoked Chicken Breast ▲ *Cream Cheese* ▲ *Jalapeño*

New York–Style Pizza Dough (page 63)

Cooked Tomato Sauce (page 27)

FOR THE SMOKED CHICKEN

1 (8-ounce) boneless, skinless chicken breast

2 tablespoons liquid smoke

1 1/2 teaspoons garlic powder

1 1/2 teaspoons extra virgin olive oil

1/2 teaspoon salt

1/4 teaspoon freshly ground black pepper

1 tablespoon extra-virgin olive oil

1/2 red onion, peeled and thinly sliced

1 tablespoon sugar

1 tablespoon red wine vinegar

8 ounces cream cheese, at room temperature

1 jalapeño pepper, seeded and chopped

This town of about 20,000 has the soul of a musician, and it's home to some major blues labels such as Fat Possum Records and Sweet Tea Studios. The Black Keys, Elvis Costello, Buddy Guy, and Bob Dylan are among the musicians who have recorded music in Oxford.

Old Venice Pizzeria has a deep Southern style blended with old-world Italian heritage. This jalapeño popper–inspired pizza with a strange name is one of the most popular pizzas on the menu. Pronounced Ban-SWAY-chee-O, this pizza has a cream cheese base, sliced chicken breast, sweet red onion, sliced jalapeño, mozzarella, and a swirl of tomato sauce.

MAKES 1 (16-INCH) PIZZA, SERVES 2 TO 3

Make the pizza dough at least 12 hours ahead. Rest the dough on the counter until it comes to room temperature, about 1 hour. Make the cooked tomato sauce.

Make the Smoked Chicken: Place the chicken breast, liquid smoke, garlic powder, olive oil, salt, and pepper in a reclosable plastic bag. Seal and shake to cover the breast. Marinate in the refrigerator for at least 1 hour or up to 12 hours.

Preheat the oven to 400°F. Place the marinated chicken breast in a small pan and bake for 15 minutes. The chicken will be only partially cooked. Let cool for 10 minutes, then cut the chicken into thin slices. Keep the oven on.

While the chicken bakes, heat the olive oil in small skillet over medium heat. Add the sliced onion, sugar, and vinegar. Cook until the onion is limp, about 5 minutes.

Increase the oven temperature to 500°F and heat for 15 minutes. Move an oven rack to the lowest position.

Shape the dough and place it on the pizza pan or screen, according to the instructions on page 64. Spread the cream cheese onto the pizza dough with a rubber spatula, leaving a 1-inch rim around the edge. Drop spoonfuls of the sautéed onion on top. Add the chicken slices and sliced jalapeño.

Spoon ½ cup of the tomato sauce into a small plastic bag (store the remaining sauce in the refrigerator for another use). Squeeze the sauce into one corner. Snip the corner to create a tiny hole and squeeze out the sauce in a thin stream, swirling it into a pattern on the top of the pizza.

Bake the pizza for about 15 minutes, until the crust is deep brown and the toppings are bubbling. Check underneath with a metal spatula to ensure the bottom crust is deep brown too. Let the pizza rest for 5 minutes. Cut it into 8 wedges and serve.

BUFFALO CHICKEN PIZZA

Buffalo Chicken ▲ *Blue Cheese* ▲ *Celery*

New York–Style Pizza Dough (page 63)

Roasted Chicken Breast (page 35)

1/4 cup Frank's RedHot sauce or Louisiana-style hot sauce

1/2 cup tomato juice

1 teaspoon cornstarch

4 tablespoons (1/2 stick) unsalted butter

2 teaspoons garlic powder

1 ounce Parmigiano Reggiano, grated (1/4 cup)

1 cup shredded mozzarella

3 ounces blue cheese, crumbled (1 cup)

1 cup sliced celery

Most people looking for a gourmet pizza might be afraid to eat in this tiny town in South Dakota. With a population of only 311 people, chances are slim that there are any skilled pizzaiolos around, right?

Rest assured that people visiting Mount Rushmore in spring, summer, or fall can get flavorful pizza at Big Time. Thousands of campers, hikers, and vacationers come to this scenic area each year, expecting to find great beauty and tranquility in nature. They are pleasantly surprised to find great pizza, too, among the rocky cliffs and mountainous terrain.

Big Time means big flavor, as in this spicy Buffalo Chicken Pizza, which just might melt the ice off that South Dakota winter. In the meantime, you can enjoy it from the comfort of your own kitchen.

MAKES 1 (16-INCH) PIZZA, SERVES 2 TO 3

Make the pizza dough at least 12 hours ahead. Rest the dough on the counter until it comes to room temperature, about 1 hour. Make the roasted chicken breast.

Move an oven rack to the lowest position. Preheat the oven to 500°F for 30 minutes.

Place the hot sauce, tomato juice, cornstarch, butter, and garlic powder in a small skillet over medium heat. Stir continuously until the sauce is smooth, about 4 minutes. Remove from the heat.

Shape the dough and place it on the pizza pan or screen, according to the instructions on page 64.

Spread the sauce on top of the pizza with a rubber spatula, leaving a 1-inch rim around the edge. Sprinkle with the Parmigiano Reggiano, leaving a 1-inch rim around the edge. Top with the mozzarella. Then add the chicken slices, crumbled blue cheese, and celery.

Bake the pizza for about 15 minutes, until the crust is deep brown and the toppings are bubbling. Check underneath with a metal spatula to ensure the bottom crust is deep brown too. Let the pizza rest for 5 minutes. Cut it into 8 wedges and serve.

HOT BROWN

Turkey ▲ Bacon ▲ Gruyère

New York–Style Pizza
    Dough (page 64)

Alfredo Sauce
    (page 30)

4¹/₂ ounces Gruyère,
    grated (1¹/₂ cups)

4   ounces bacon
    (4 strips)

12 ounces sliced
    cooked turkey
    breast

1   small tomato,
    chopped

1   tablespoon chopped
    fresh flat-leaf
    parsley

Louisville is home to the Kentucky Derby, the prestigious annual horse race that, since 1875, has drawn thousands of people every year. Many grand hotels opened to accommodate the visitors, including the Brown Hotel in 1923. Chef Fred Schmidt created the hotel's signature dish, the Hot Brown sandwich, now a Louisville tradition. Roast turkey, bacon, and tomato are covered in a creamy sauce with Gruyère and broiled until hot and brown.

Benny Impellizzeri began selling his distinctive pizzas, made with two layers of toppings and two layers of cheese, from his dad's butcher shop in 1978. They later became known as "Louisville-style" pizzas. Impellizzeri's has done a fine job of honoring Louisville cuisine with its creamy, rich Hot Brown pizza.

MAKES 1 (16-INCH) PIZZA, SERVES 3 TO 4

Make the pizza dough at least 12 hours ahead. Rest the dough on the counter until it comes to room temperature, about 1 hour.

Preheat the oven to 400°F.

Make the alfredo sauce. Before it cools, add 1 cup of the grated Gruyère and keep stirring as the cheese melts into the sauce.

Place the bacon strips on a small pan and bake for 15 minutes. They will be partially cooked. Drain on paper towels. Let cool, then slice into 1-inch pieces.

Move an oven rack to the lowest position. Increase the oven temperature to 500°F and heat for 15 minutes.

Shape the dough and place it on the pizza pan or screen, according to the instructions on page 64. Spread the sauce on the dough with a rubber spatula, leaving a 1-inch border around the edge. Sprinkle with the remaining ¹/₂ cup grated Gruyère. Top with the turkey slices, followed by the bacon.

Bake the pizza for 18 to 20 minutes, until the crust is deep brown and the toppings are bubbling. Check underneath with a metal spatula to ensure the bottom crust is deep brown too. Let the pizza rest for 5 minutes. Sprinkle with the chopped tomato and parsley, then cut the pizza into 8 wedges and serve.

SHRIMP SCAMPI PIZZA

Shrimp ▲ *Garlic Butter* ▲ *Panko Breadcrumbs*

SANTARPIO'S,
BOSTON,
MASSACHUSETTS

This East Coast institution has been serving Bostonians since 1903. The place is filled with thick Boston accents and Frank Sinatra on the jukebox. The pie features jumbo shrimp slathered in rich garlic butter on a bed of fresh mozzarella. Shrimp scampi is the Italian-American dish in which shrimp are baked in garlic butter and nestled under a bed of bread crumbs and cheese. It's all that and more on a pizza.

New York–Style Pizza Dough (page 63)

FOR THE SCAMPI

4 tablespoons (1/2 stick) unsalted butter

4 cloves garlic, minced

Zest and juice of 1 lemon

2 tablespoons chopped fresh flat-leaf parsley

1 teaspoon salt

1/2 teaspoon freshly ground black pepper

1 pound peeled, deveined shrimp (16 to 20 count)

1 ounce Parmigiano Reggiano, grated (1/4 cup)

8 ounces fresh mozzarella, thinly sliced

1/2 cup panko bread crumbs

1 tablespoon extra-virgin olive oil

1 tablespoon chopped fresh flat-leaf parsley

MAKES 1 (16-INCH) PIZZA, SERVES 2 TO 3

Make the pizza dough at least 12 hours ahead. Rest the dough on the counter until it comes to room temperature, about 1 hour.

Move an oven rack to the lowest position. Preheat the oven to 500°F for 30 minutes.

Make the Scampi: Melt the butter in a medium skillet over medium-high heat. Add the garlic, lemon zest and juice, parsley, salt, pepper, and shrimp and stir for 1 minute. Turn off the heat. The shrimp will be partially cooked. Add the Parmigiano Reggiano and stir.

Shape the dough and place it on the pizza pan or screen, according to the instructions on page 64. Top with the sliced mozzarella, leaving a 1-inch border around the edge. Add the shrimp. Drizzle the garlic butter over the pizza. Sprinkle the panko on top and drizzle with the olive oil.

Bake the pizza for 15 to 20 minutes, until the crust is deep brown and the toppings are bubbling. Check underneath with a metal spatula to ensure the bottom crust is deep brown too. Let the pizza rest for 5 minutes. Sprinkle the pizza with the chopped parsley, then cut it into 8 wedges and serve.

Chapter 5

SICILIAN-STYLE PIZZAS

Sicilian pizza hails from Palermo, the capital of Sicily. It evolved from focaccia, which is even more ancient than pizza. Sometimes called *sfincione*, it is made in a square or oblong pan. This pizza has a thick crust with a crispy bottom. It is typically topped sparingly with light sauce or grated hard cheeses. Originally, it was a peasant food used to stretch a small amount of hard cheese or herbs and tomatoes.

Today, some American pizzerias still create the authentic square pizza, a thick, spongy pie topped with a thin layer of tomato sauce, olive oil, and cheese. But baking pans in New York City were rectangular, so many went in that direction. Sicilian immigrants settled in Detroit and created the famous Detroit Red Stripe. Sometimes they are called Grandma pizzas on the East Coast, where Sicilian pizza is most popular. Grandmas have a little more cheese. There's a Grandpa pizza too—a deceptively simple pizza with crispy bread crumbs. There's also a well-known Sicilian pizza in Wyoming, of all places.

SICILIAN-STYLE PIZZA DOUGH

4 cups all-purpose flour

1¹/₂ cups warm water

1¹/₂ tablespoons active dry yeast

1 tablespoon extra-virgin olive oil, plus more as needed

1 teaspoon sugar

1¹/₂ teaspoons salt

This flavorful dough creates a thick, spongy crust that's full of air. The crust comes out tender yet firm. The dough is kneaded less than the other pizza doughs, which makes the crust more cakelike and tender. Because it's baked in a metal pan with sides and lots of oil on the bottom, it comes out crispy. You can make it in either a rectangular sheet pan or a square Sicilian pan.

Make this dough up to three days in advance. Because it's a large amount of dough, it needs to rest on the counter for up to two hours to come to room temperature.

MAKES DOUGH FOR 1 (18 X 12¹/₂-INCH OR 15 X 15-INCH) PIZZA

Place the flour, water, yeast, olive oil, and sugar in the bowl of a stand mixer fitted with the dough hook. Mix on low to combine, about 1 minute.

Turn off the mixer and let the dough rest for about 10 minutes. Add the salt and 1 or 2 teaspoons of cool water if the dough looks a little dry. Knead the dough on medium speed for about 5 minutes, until the dough is smooth and supple.

Pour a teaspoon of olive oil into a medium bowl. Shape the dough into a ball and place it in the bowl. Turn the dough to coat it with the oil. This prevents a crust from forming on its surface as

it rises. Cover the bowl with plastic wrap and let the dough rise in the refrigerator for at least 12 hours and up to 72 hours. After 12 hours, the dough will have doubled in volume. Rest the dough on the counter until it comes to room temperature, at least 2 hours.

Choosing the Pan: You can make a rectangular pizza that fills an 18 x 12¹/₂ x 1-inch half sheet pan (page 15), or a 15 x 15-inch pizza that fills a square pan (page 15). If you like a thicker crust, use the square pan. It also makes a more traditional pizza.

Get the Dough in Shape

STRETCH THE DOUGH USING A HALF SHEET OR SQUARE PIZZA PAN Oil the entire pan with 2 tablespoons of olive oil. Place the dough in the pan and gently pat it down using your fingers.

Bring it up onto the side of the pan to build a little wall around the border. Your Sicilian-style dough is now ready for the toppings.

BLT PIZZA

Bacon ▲ Arugula ▲ Tomato Sauce

Sicilian-Style Pizza Dough (page 86)

Chunky Tomato Sauce (page 27)

1/4 cup grated Parmigiano Reggiano

2 cups shredded mozzarella

12 ounces bacon (12 strips)

1/2 cup ricotta

4 ounces baby arugula (about 4 cups)

2 tablespoons balsamic vinegar

1 1/2 tablespoons extra-virgin olive oil

Pinch of salt

Pinch of freshly ground black pepper

Pizza entrepreneurs Brian Somershield and Geoff Lockert thought Birmingham was an excellent place to set up a pizzeria called Trattoria Centrale—and they were right. Birmingham, named after the city in England, is the cultural and entertainment capital of Alabama. The railroad brought major businesses to Birmingham and guaranteed its growth.

Since 2009, Trattoria Centrale has grown too, serving Sicilian-style pizzas and Italian entrées. Pizza is always on the menu and sold by the square slice. This one arrives with a green salad on top, with a balsamic vinegar dressing that complements the richness of the pizza, with its bacon and three kinds of cheese.

MAKES 1 (15 X 15-INCH) PIZZA, SERVES 5 TO 6

Make the pizza dough at least 12 hours ahead. Rest the dough on the counter until it comes to room temperature, at least 2 hours. Make the chunky tomato sauce at least 1 hour ahead.

Preheat the oven to 400°F.

Place the bacon strips on a small pan and bake for 15 minutes. They will be partially cooked. Drain on paper towels. Let cool, then slice into 1-inch pieces.

Move an oven rack to the lowest position. Increase the oven temperature to 500°F and heat for 15 minutes.

Shape the dough on a 15 x 15-inch square pan, according to the instructions on page 86. Sprinkle with the Parmigiano Reggiano and mozzarella. Drop spoonfuls of the tomato sauce on the pizza, followed by spoonfuls of ricotta. Sprinkle with the chopped bacon.

Bake the pizza for about 20 minutes, until the toppings are bubbling and the crust is a deep brown. Let the pizza rest for 5 minutes.

Toss the arugula in a large bowl with the vinegar, olive oil, salt, and pepper. Distribute the salad over the pizza and cut it into 16 squares.

GRANDMA PIZZA

Sausage ▲ Broccoli Rabe ▲ Parmigiano Reggiano

Sicilian-Style Pizza Dough (page 86)

New York–Style Pizza Sauce (page 28), doubled

1 tablespoon salt

2 cups shredded mozzarella

12 ounces mild Italian sausage meat

12 ounces broccoli rabe (about 1 bunch)

2 ounces Parmigiano Reggiano, grated ($1/2$ cup)

Umberto Corteo learned how to make pizza as a boy in Naples, Italy. His brother Joe came with him to America, where the two boys started Umberto's. There they introduced the Grandma pizza, based on a Sicilian crust. The name stuck. The Grandma pizza is always a large rectangular pizza, about 18 by 12 inches. It's usually just tomato sauce and cheese, or sometimes it has a dark green vegetable like broccoli rabe or sausage. This pizza uses both broccoli rabe and sausage to make a big, comforting pizza. The bitterness of the rabe contrasts beautifully with the flavors of fennel and garlic in the sausage.

Now you can find Grandma pizza all over New York, but Umberto's has the best. That is, until you try this one at home.

MAKES 1 (18 X 12$1/2$-INCH) PIZZA, SERVES 5 TO 6

Make the pizza dough at least 24 hours ahead. Rest the dough on the counter until it comes to room temperature, at least 2 hours. Make the pizza sauce at least 1 hour ahead.

Move an oven rack to the lowest position. Preheat the oven to 500°F for 30 minutes.

Fill a large pot halfway with water and add the salt. Bring to a boil over high heat. Add the broccoli rabe and boil for about 5 minutes, until tender. Prepare a large bowl of ice water. Transfer the broccoli rabe to the ice water to stop the cooking and cool it off quickly. Pick up the broccoli rabe and squeeze out the excess water. Chop it into 1-inch pieces.

Shape the dough on an 18 x 12$1/2$-inch half sheet pan, according to the instructions on page 86. Spread the pizza sauce on the dough with a rubber spatula, leaving a $1/2$-inch border. Sprinkle with the mozzarella. Drop teaspoonfuls of the raw sausage on top. Distribute the broccoli rabe over the pizza. Sprinkle the Parmigiano Reggiano all over.

Bake the pizza for about 20 minutes, until the toppings are bubbling and the crust is a deep brown. Let the pizza rest for 5 minutes. Cut it into 16 pieces and serve.

GRANDPA PIZZA

Red Onion ▲ Bread Crumbs ▲ Parmigiano Reggiano

PAPPARDELLE'S PIZZERIA, BETHPAGE, NEW YORK

Sicilian-Style Pizza Dough (page 86)

New York–Style Pizza Sauce (page 28), doubled

2 cups shredded mozzarella

1 cup sliced red onion

1/2 cup Italian seasoned bread crumbs

1 ounce grated Parmigiano Reggiano (1/4 cup)

When the Grandma pizza became popular, the only logical thing to do was to make a Grandpa pie, a simple rectangular pie with seasoned bread crumbs on top to make it extra crispy. They remind me of the bristly whiskers of my granddad, who would hug me in a wine-scented bear hug and rub his sandpapery face on mine. Make some more memories when you make this pizza, and don't forget the hugs.

MAKES 1 (18 X 12¹/₂-INCH) PIZZA, SERVES 5 TO 6

Make the pizza dough at least 24 hours ahead. Rest the dough on the counter until it comes to room temperature, at least 2 hours. Make the pizza sauce at least 1 hour ahead.

Move an oven rack to the lowest position. Preheat the oven to 500°F for 30 minutes.

Shape the dough on an 18 x 12¹/₂-inch half sheet pan, according to the instructions on page 86. Spread the pizza sauce on the dough with a

rubber spatula, leaving a ¹/₂-inch border. Sprinkle with the mozzarella, onion, and bread crumbs. Sprinkle the Parmigiano Reggiano around the edges.

Bake the pizza for about 20 minutes, until the toppings are bubbling and the crust is a deep brown. Let the pizza rest for 5 minutes. Cut it into 16 pieces and serve.

SICILIAN BACON CHEESEBURGER PIZZA

Ground Beef ▲ *Cheddar* ▲ *Dill Pickle*

Sicilian-Style Pizza
  Dough (page 86)

Chunky Tomato Sauce
  (page 27)

1 pound ground beef

1 teaspoon celery salt

1 teaspoon dry
   mustard

1 teaspoon garlic
   powder

1/2 teaspoon salt

1 teaspoon freshly
   ground black
   pepper

1 cup shredded
   mozzarella

2 cups shredded
   cheddar

1/2 cup dill pickle
   chips, cut into thin
   strips

1/4 cup diced red onion

THE PIZZA PLACE,
LUSK, WYOMING

The Black Hills gold rush of 1874 brought
Frank Lusk to Wyoming, and led to the creation
of the town, later named after him. Today the
city is built on ranching and raising cattle. Do
you know how hungry these folks get, ranching
cattle all day? They need good pizza in Lusk.

Fortunately, they have it. At the Pizza Place,
guests are heard to say, "I never expected to
have pizza this good in the middle of nowhere."
Happily, you don't have to saddle up your
horse. Stay home and make this Sicilian Bacon
Cheeseburger Pizza. It combines the best of two
of America's favorite foods in one thick pie,
and tastes just like a burger, with cheddar, red
onion, and dill pickle chips on top of seasoned
ground beef.

MAKES 1 (18 X 12½-INCH) PIZZA, SERVES 5 TO 6

Make the pizza dough at least 24 hours ahead.
Rest the dough on the counter until it comes to
room temperature, at least 2 hours. Make the
chunky tomato sauce at least I hour ahead.

Move an oven rack to the lowest position.
Preheat the oven to 500°F for 30 minutes.

Place the ground beef in a medium skillet over
medium-high heat. Break up the beef with a
spoon and stir in the celery salt, dry mustard, garlic powder, salt, and pepper. Cook until browned,
about 5 minutes.

Shape the dough on an 18 x 12½-inch half sheet
pan, according to the instructions on page 86.
Spread the tomato sauce on the dough with a
rubber spatula, leaving a ½-inch border. Sprinkle
with the mozzarella. Distribute the cooked beef
over the top and sprinkle with the cheddar.

Bake the pizza for about 20 minutes, until the
crust is a deep brown and the toppings are bubbling. Let the pizza rest for 5 minutes. Sprinkle
with the pickle strips and diced onion, then cut
into 16 pieces and serve.

THE PALERMO

Caramelized Onions ▲ Bread Crumbs ▲ Parmigiano Reggiano

Sicilian-Style Pizza Dough (page 86)

Cooked Tomato Sauce (page 27)

1/4 cup plus 2 tablespoons extra-virgin olive oil

4 medium yellow onions, peeled and thinly sliced

1 teaspoon salt

3/4 cup bread crumbs

1 ounce Parmigiano Reggiano, grated (1/4 cup)

If you don't like surly Italians serving you pizza, go somewhere else. But what you might call surly, I call character. New York should be a little gritty. This place has grit, and probably the best slice of Sicilian pizza outside of Sicily.

This recipe will stretch your vision of pizza. It is light and airy, crispy and oily, but there is no gooey cheese or plentiful sauce. This is an old-world Sicilian pie, more like focaccia. Try it with an Italian salad and a side of calamari.

MAKES 1 (15 X 15-INCH) PIZZA, SERVES 5 TO 6

Make the pizza dough at least 24 hours ahead. Rest the dough on the counter until it comes to room temperature, at least 2 hours. Make the cooked tomato sauce.

Move an oven rack to the lowest position. Preheat the oven to 500°F for 30 minutes.

Heat 1/4 cup of the olive oil over medium heat in a medium skillet. Add the onions and cook, stirring frequently, until golden brown, about 20 minutes. Add the salt and stir. Let cool for about 10 minutes.

Shape the dough on a 15 x 15-inch sheet pan, according to the instructions on page 86. Spread the tomato sauce over the dough with a rubber spatula, leaving a 1/2-inch border. Distribute the onions over the sauce. Mix the bread crumbs with the Parmigiano Reggiano and the remaining 2 tablespoons olive oil in a small bowl. Sprinkle over the pizza and pat the crumbs down gently with your fingers.

Bake the pizza for about 20 minutes, until the toppings are bubbling and the crust is a deep brown. Let the pizza rest for 5 minutes. Cut it into 16 squares and serve.

CRAB PIZZA

Fresh Crab ▲ Roasted Zucchini ▲ Egg

JOE SQUARED,
BALTIMORE, MARYLAND

Sicilian-Style Pizza Dough (page 86)

Roasted Zucchini (page 34)

Alfredo Sauce (page 30)

2 ounces Parmigiano Reggiano, grated (1/2 cup)

1 cup shredded mozzarella

2 ounces cheddar, shredded (1/4 cup)

8 ounces cooked crabmeat

1/4 cup sliced red onion

4 eggs

1/2 cup chopped fresh cilantro (from about 1/2 bunch)

Joe Squared is famous for its tasty coal-fired square pizzas. The pizza features ultra-modern toppings, capitalizing on the recent trend of putting an egg on everything. The combination of crab, zucchini, and egg with a rich cheese sauce is unusual, but it works. The silky yolk ties together the sweet crab and earthy zucchini. A topping of round yellow yolks and round green zucchini slices makes it unexpectedly beautiful.

MAKES 1 (15 X 15-INCH) PIZZA, SERVES 5 TO 6

Make the pizza dough at least 24 hours ahead. Rest the dough on the counter until it comes to room temperature, at least 2 hours.

Make the roasted zucchini. Move an oven rack to the lowest position. Increase the oven temperature to 500°F and let it heat for 15 minutes.

Make the alfredo sauce. Before it cools, add 1/4 cup of the Parmigiano Reggiano, and keep stirring as the cheese melts into the sauce.

Shape the dough on a 15 x 15-inch square pan, according to the instructions on page 86. Spread the sauce over the dough with a rubber spatula,

all the way out to the edges. Sprinkle with the remaining 1/4 cup Parmigiano Reggiano, the mozzarella, and the cheddar. Place the zucchini rounds evenly on top, followed by the crab. Top with the onion.

Bake the pizza for 10 minutes. Open the oven door flat and pull out the rack partway. Carefully crack the eggs over the center of the pizza. Bake until the toppings are bubbling and the crust is deep brown, about 5 minutes more. Remove the pizza when the eggs are still soft. Let the pizza rest for 5 minutes. Sprinkle with the cilantro, then cut into 16 squares and serve.

RED STRIPE PIZZA

Pizza Sauce ▲ Cheddar ▲ Pecorino Romano ▲ Mozzarella ▲ Jack

Sicilian-Style Pizza Dough (page 86)

New York–Style Pizza Sauce (page 28), doubled

3 ounces Pecorino Romano, shredded (¼ cup)

1 cup shredded cheddar

1 cup shredded mozzarella

1 cup shredded Jack or brick cheese

BUDDY'S RESTAURANT AND PIZZERIA, DETROIT, MICHIGAN

The year was 1936. Buddy's Pizza was a blind pig, which means it started as an underground business and skirted state and federal laws governing on-site sales and alcohol consumption. While Buddy's sold booze, the owner didn't build his fame on liquor. He made a great pizza too.

In Detroit, the post–World War I automotive industry was huge. Auto racing was even bigger. So Buddy painted two wide stripes of sauce down the middle of his square pizza to signify the burnt rubber peel out on pavement. Detroit's Red Stripe Square Pizza was born, a simple four-cheese pizza with a crunchy burned cheese topping and a zesty sauce.

MAKES 1 (15 X 15-INCH) PIZZA, SERVES 5 TO 6

Make the pizza dough at least 24 hours ahead. Rest the dough on the counter until it comes to room temperature, at least 2 hours. Make the pizza sauce at least 1 hour ahead.

Move an oven rack to the lowest position. Preheat the oven to 500°F for 30 minutes.

Shape the dough on a 15 x 15-inch square pan, according to the instructions on page 86. Sprinkle with the Romano, followed by the cheddar, mozzarella, and Jack, sprinkling them out to the edge of the pan. The cheese must touch the pan sides to get the characteristic crunchy and blackened edges.

Using a ladle, make 2- to 3-inch-wide stripes of pizza sauce down the middle of the pizza. Do not spread the sauce.

Bake the pizza for about 20 minutes, until the top is browned and the edges are black and crispy. Let the pizza rest for 5 minutes. Cut it into 16 squares and serve.

Chapter 6

SOURDOUGH PIZZAS

Sourdough pizza crust? It may not have occurred to you. You are probably thinking of the super-sour French bread from San Francisco, but this crust is not that bread. This crust is light, airy, and mildly tangy, with a shiny top and a crispy bottom.

Sourdough simply means it's made from a wild yeast culture. Some people think sourdough goes back to Egyptian times. Europeans have baked with sourdough for centuries. The most famous American sourdough maker is the Boudin family, master bakers from France who moved to San Francisco more than 150 years ago. The bakery has used the same sourdough starter since 1849.

The restaurants showcased in this chapter have been making sourdough pizza crusts for years. Most are based in the Midwest and the South, which surprised me. Only one San Francisco sourdough pizza, from Delfina, was good enough to include.

It's a bit of a project to make this dough, but once you have a starter, you're set to make fantastic sourdough pizza dough whenever you like.

SOURDOUGH PIZZA DOUGH BASICS

The sourdough pizza crust is not sour, but a little tangy and chewy. It is one of the most sophisticated doughs to make, but worth the steps. It rewards you with a thin, crispy layer on top and puffy dough inside.

Sourdough pizza dough requires making a liquid starter as a substitute for dry yeast. Keep your starter alive forever in the fridge, if you wish, and use it for bread or pancakes—or, best of all, more pizza.

The starter needs wild yeast, not the commercially raised yeast sold at the grocery store. This wild yeast is centuries old and carries bacteria that supports the yeast functions and develops flavor. I bought mine from Sourdoughs International, www.sourdo.com, which carries fine wild yeast cultures from all over the world. I prefer the Italian sourdough cultures. They are among the best I have ever tried, consistently producing vibrant, flavorful pizzas with a rich, slightly sour taste. Sourdoughs International also provides a wealth of information about making sourdough products.

SOURDOUGH STARTER

1 sourdough culture
  packet

1 cup room
  temperature water

1 cup unbleached all-
  purpose flour

Sourdough starter is a small fermented dough. While it's not a difficult process, and the results are rewarding, it must be made five days prior to making pizza—so plan ahead! All you have to do is feed the starter daily, keep it warm, and watch it bubble and ferment. The result is a product you can use for decades.

Pour the sourdough culture into a clean, I-quart mason jar with lid and ring. Add the water and flour, and screw the lid on, but not too tightly so a little gas can escape. Shake the jar until the contents are well mixed, and find a warm place to keep it, where the temperature ranges between 70° and 90°F. This could be your oven (if it has a gas pilot light), the top of your refrigerator, or on top of electronic equipment.

Feeding your starter: Every day for 5 days, feed your starter to keep it fresh and to prevent yeast-killing acids from building up. To do this, pour out I cup of starter. Add 1/2 cup room temperature water and 1/2 cup unbleached all-purpose flour. Seal it—again not too tightly so a little gas can escape—and shake.

After 2 or 3 days you will see active fermentation: bubbles will appear and the starter will rise. If the liquid separates or deflates, it could be a lag stage, which will transform when you feed the starter again. (If the starter smells like ammonia, it has gone bad. Discard it and start again.) The most important indicator is the texture. You want

the starter to be as thick as sour cream. If it is not, add more flour to thicken it, a teaspoon at a time. Two or three teaspoons should be enough. The jar should be a little less than half full at all times to give the yeast room to grow when it's actively feeding.

On the fifth day, your starter is ready to use. That day, feed the starter 2 hours before you make your dough. It should be active and full of bubbles when you add it to the dough.

Once you've used your starter, either keep it alive indefinitely to make more pizzas, or put the starter to sleep until you need it. To keep your starter alive, keep feeding it every 2 or 3 days as described. To keep the starter dormant for future use, just put it in the fridge. It will stay dormant for months or even years. Some insist on a monthly feeding, but I have left mine alone. To activate your refrigerated starter, begin 2 days before you need the starter. For 2 days, feed the starter as indicated in the instructions above, until it starts rising and bubbling again.

SOURDOUGH PIZZA DOUGH

4¹/2 cups unbleached flour, plus more as needed

1 cup active Sourdough Starter (page 101)

2 tablespoons sugar

1 tablespoon extra-virgin olive oil, plus more for hands and countertop

1¹/2 cups water

2 teaspoons salt

Sourdough pizza dough is wet, stretchy, and elastic. You'll need to oil your hands and the countertop to get it out of the bowl and form the balls of dough. This recipe makes enough dough for two pizzas. You don't want to make the starter for only one pizza! You can freeze the other ball for up to 3 months in a freezer bag.

Start the dough two days before you're ready to use it. The dough rises so slowly it needs that time in the fridge to develop flavor. It lasts in the fridge for up to five days, and it will rise a little more on the counter when you bring it to room temperature.

MAKES DOUGH FOR 2 (14-INCH) PIZZAS

Place the flour, starter, sugar, oil, and water into the bowl of a stand mixer fitted with the dough hook. Mix on low to combine, about 2 minutes.

Turn off the mixer and let the dough rest for about 10 minutes. Add the salt, and knead the dough on medium speed for about 15 minutes, until the dough is wet, sticky, and elastic. If the dough seems too wet, sticky, and soft, add 1 or 2 tablespoons flour, just until the dough is supple and drier.

To test elasticity, hold a 1-inch piece between your fingers and stretch the dough to make a windowpane. It should look like bubblegum. If not, knead for 5 minutes more and test again. Keep going until the dough passes the test, up to 30 minutes more.

Oil your hands and spread a little oil onto a clean countertop. Transfer the dough to the oiled counter and divide it into 2 equal pieces. Roll each piece into a ball by pinching the bottom of the dough together and rounding the dough, until it has a tight bottom without creases. Turn the balls to coat them with the oil. Place the balls on a tray or sheet pan with raised sides, cover with plastic, and refrigerate for 24 hours to develop flavor. The dough will flatten out and will not rise much. Rest the dough on the counter until it comes to room temperature, about 2 hours.

Get the Dough in Shape

STRETCH THE DOUGH Make dimples in the dough ball with your fingertips by pressing down in the middle to stretch it out. At the same time, move the dough around in a circle with your fingertips. A 1-inch rim should form naturally. Press your fingertips along the inside of the rim, moving in a circle. Place your hands on the dough, fingers up against the rim, and push out while turning in a circle. Add more flour if necessary, to ensure the dough slides easily.

Pick up the dough to finish stretching it out. Slide your hands underneath it and pick it up. Let the dough fall around your hands to stretch it. Keep your hands along the edges, rather than in the middle. The dough should be 14 inches in diameter.

PLACE THE DOUGH ON THE PAN OR SCREEN Spray a 14-inch pizza pan with nonstick cooking spray and then lightly coat with flour. Place the pan next to the dough on the counter and quickly pick up the dough while sliding it onto the pan. Reshape as necessary in a round or oval shape. Your sourdough pizza dough is now ready for the toppings.

MEATBALL MANIA

Meatballs ▲ Cincinnati Sweet Red Sauce ▲ Banana Peppers

Sourdough Pizza
Dough (page 102)

Nonstick cooking spray

FOR THE ITALIAN MEATBALLS

$1/2$ pound ground beef

$1/2$ pound ground pork

1 egg

$1/4$ cup milk

$1/2$ cup bread crumbs

$1/2$ teaspoon salt

1 teaspoon dried oregano

1 tablespoon chopped fresh flat-leaf parsley

3 cloves garlic, chopped

$1/2$ teaspoon freshly ground black pepper

1 ounce Parmigiano Reggiano, grated ($1/4$ cup)

FOR THE CINCINNATI SWEET RED SAUCE

Cooked Tomato Sauce (page 27)

2 tablespoons minced onion

1 tablespoon finely grated carrot

1 tablespoon honey

2 tablespoons dark brown sugar

1 ounce grated Parmigiano Reggiano ($1/4$ cup)

2 cups shredded mozzarella

$1/4$ cup pickled banana peppers

1 tablespoon dried oregano

7 fresh basil leaves, shredded

About twenty years ago, a businessman, an accountant, a minister, and a football player teamed up with a farmer, a surgeon, a schoolteacher, a banker, a homemaker, a principal, and a produce salesman. I know, it sounds like the beginning of a joke, but together they created an iconic pizza business in Cincinnati.

Pizza Tower has helped spread the fame of Cincinnati-style pizza, a hand-tossed pie with a sweet tomato sauce. Meatball Mania includes a red sauce with brown sugar, something most pizzaiolos would never do, but boy it's good. Add tangy banana peppers and meatballs and you've got an irresistible combination, cooked like a regular pizza.

MAKES 1 (14-INCH) PIZZA, SERVES 3 TO 4

Make the pizza dough at least 2 days ahead. Rest 1 ball of dough on the counter until it comes to room temperature, about 2 hours.

Preheat the oven to 400°F. Spray a large sheet pan with nonstick cooking spray.

Make the Italian Meatballs: In a medium bowl, gently mix the beef, pork, egg, milk, bread crumbs, salt, oregano, parsley, garlic, black pepper, and

Parmigiano Reggiano until combined. Don't overmix or the meatballs will be tough. Divide the spiced meat into 24 pieces. Roll each piece between the palms of your hands to form a ball and place on the prepared sheet pan. Bake for 15 to 20 minutes, until browned and fully cooked.

Move an oven rack to the lowest position. Increase the oven temperature to 500°F and heat for 15 minutes.

Make the Cincinatti Sweet Red Sauce: To the cooked tomato sauce, add the onion, carrot, honey, and brown sugar after the tomato puree, and cook as directed in the recipe.

Shape the dough and place it on the pizza pan or screen, according to the instructions on page 103. Spread the sauce on the dough with a rubber spatula, leaving a 1/2-inch border. Sprinkle with the Parmigiano Reggiano and mozzarella, and

place the meatballs on top. Sprinkle with the banana peppers and oregano.

Bake the pizza for 15 to 20 minutes, until the crust is deep brown and the toppings are bubbling. Check underneath with a metal spatula to ensure the bottom crust is deep brown too. Let the pizza rest for 5 minutes. Sprinkle the pizza with the basil, then cut it into 8 wedges and serve.

SHEER DELIGHT PIZZA

Portobellos ▲ Gorgonzola ▲ Sesame Seeds

Sourdough Pizza Dough (page 102)

Pesto Sauce (page 30)

2 portobello mushrooms

2 tablespoons extra-virgin olive oil

1 ounce grated Parmigiano Reggiano (¹/₄ cup)

6 ounces fresh mozzarella

¹/₂ cup walnut pieces

3 ounces Gorgonzola

1 egg, beaten

2 tablespoons sesame seeds

ASHEVILLE BREWING COMPANY, ASHEVILLE, NORTH CAROLINA

This small city has a strong tradition of street fests and outdoor music. People there love to dance, drink, and eat pizza. Who doesn't?

They might grab a pint and order this pie at Asheville Brewing Company. This pie has a big fat rim loaded with toasted sesame seeds. It makes your crust look and taste like a big crispy sesame stick. You'll love how well it pairs with pesto, Gorgonzola, and portobello mushrooms.

MAKES 1 (14-INCH) PIZZA, SERVES 3 TO 4

Make the pizza dough at least 2 days ahead. Rest 1 ball of the dough on the counter until it comes to room temperature, about 2 hours. Make the pesto sauce.

Move an oven rack to the lowest position. Preheat the oven to 500°F for 30 minutes.

Prepare the mushrooms by scraping out the black gills with a spoon and discarding them. Cut the mushrooms into ¹/₄-inch slices. Sauté in the olive oil in a medium skillet over medium-high heat for about 5 minutes, until the mushrooms are limp and cooked through.

Shape the dough and place it on the screen, according to the instructions on page 103. Spread the pesto sauce on the dough with a rubber spatula, leaving a ¹/₂-inch border. Sprinkle with the Parmigiano Reggiano. Tear the mozzarella into small pieces and scatter them over the pizza. Follow with the mushrooms and walnut pieces. Crumble the Gorgonzola and scatter the pieces over the top. Brush the rim of the dough with the egg, and sprinkle the sesame seeds around the rim. Press lightly on the seeds to ensure they stick to the dough.

Bake the pizza on the bottom rack for about 20 minutes, until the crust is deep brown and the toppings are bubbling. Check underneath with a metal spatula to ensure the bottom crust is deep brown too. Let the pizza rest for 5 minutes. Cut it into 8 wedges and serve.

CHILI PIE

Chili ▲ Cheddar ▲ Sour Cream

Sourdough Pizza Dough (page 102)

1   pound ground beef

1   (1.25-ounce) package chili seasoning mix

1   (14¹/2-ounce) can diced tomatoes

1   (14¹/2-ounce) can pinto or kidney beans, drained and rinsed

1   (16-ounce bag) shredded cheddar (2 cups)

¹/2   cup sour cream

¹/2   cup diced red onion

1   tablespoon chopped fresh flat-leaf parsley

STREETZA PIZZA, MILWAUKEE, WISCONSIN

This simple pizza was inspired by a Milwaukee food truck hot enough to be on the Food Network. The pizza is covered in chili and shredded cheddar, and streaked with sour cream for a cooling, rich touch. It makes a hearty meal in winter.

MAKES 1 (14-INCH) PIZZA, SERVES 3 TO 4

Make the pizza dough at least 2 days ahead. Rest 1 ball of the dough on the counter until it comes to room temperature, about 2 hours.

Move an oven rack to the lowest position. Preheat the oven to 500˚F for 30 minutes.

Brown the ground beef over medium-high heat in a medium skillet, about 4 minutes. Stir in the seasoning mix, tomatoes, and beans and bring to a boil. Reduce the heat to low and simmer for about 15 minutes, until thick and the liquid has evaporated.

Shape the dough and place it on the pizza pan or screen, according to the instructions on page 103. Sprinkle with 1 cup of the shredded cheddar. Spread the chili on top with a rubber spatula, leaving a ¹/2-inch border, followed by the remaining 1 cup shredded cheddar.

Bake the pizza for 15 to 20 minutes, until the crust is deep brown and the toppings are bubbling. Check underneath with a metal spatula to ensure the bottom crust is deep brown too. Let the pizza rest for 5 minutes.

Spoon the sour cream into a small plastic bag. Squeeze the sauce into one corner. Snip the corner to produce a tiny hole and squeeze out the sour cream in a thin stream. Swirl it back and forth over the whole pizza. Sprinkle the pizza with the red onion and parsley, then cut it into 8 wedges and serve.

STATE FAIR PIZZA

Sausage ▲ *Onion* ▲ *Mustard*

Sourdough Pizza
  Dough (page 102)

Roasted Red Pepper
  Strips (page 32)

1 tablespoon butter

1 tablespoon extra-
   virgin olive oil

1 large onion, peeled
   and thinly sliced

4 ounces Gulden's
   Brown Mustard

2 cups shredded
   mozzarella

8 ounces mild Italian
   sausage, casings
   removed

A barrage of nostalgia must've hit the pizza makers at Bottoms Up when they created this pie. The State Fair pizza captures the essence of the state fair with grilled sausage and caramelized onions, and a tangy mustard sauce baked right into the pizza. Its mouthwatering smell reminds me of the quick-serve grill stands that dot the fairgrounds. Enjoy a day at the state fair.

MAKES 1 (14-INCH) PIZZA, SERVES 3 TO 4

Make the pizza dough at least 2 days ahead. Rest I ball of the dough on the counter until it comes to room temperature, about 2 hours. Make the roasted red pepper strips.

Move an oven rack to the lowest position. Preheat the oven to 500°F for 30 minutes.

Heat the butter and olive oil in a medium skillet, over medium-high heat. Add the sliced onion and cook until golden brown, stirring frequently, about I0 minutes.

Shape the dough and place it on the screen, according to the instructions on page I03. Spread the mustard on the dough with a rubber spatula, leaving a I-inch border. Top with the caramelized onion and sprinkle with the mozzarella. Drop spoonfuls of the raw sausage on top and distribute the roasted red peppers over all.

Bake the pizza for about 20 minutes, until the crust is deep brown and the toppings are bubbling. Check underneath with a metal spatula to ensure the bottom crust is deep brown too. Let the pizza rest for 5 minutes. Cut it into 8 wedges and serve.

NUCCI PIZZA

Arugula ▲ *Capicola* ▲ *Green Olives*

Sourdough Pizza Dough (page 102)

Herbed Olive Oil (page 31)

4 cloves garlic, minced

1 tablespoon minced fresh basil leaves

2 ounces grated Parmigiano Reggiano ($^1/_2$ cup)

2 tablespoons chopped green olives

8 ounces shredded Emmenthaler or Swiss cheese (2 cups)

4 ounces baby arugula (about 4 cups)

3 ounces thinly sliced capicola

$^1/_4$ cup good-quality balsamic vinegar

Jeff Varasano once made English muffin pizzas in his toaster oven. He went on to become a sought-after pizza expert, studying pizza-making techniques for ten years. His restaurant, Varasano's, opened in 2009 in the affluent Atlanta neighborhood of Buckhead. He hosts pizza tastings in his own home, and people from all over the world fly to Atlanta to attend.

Luckily, you don't have to wait. The Varasano approach is always to apply simple ingredients without fanfare, but in the most effective way possible. Here, he tops a bed of peppery raw arugula with room temperature capicola, which melts on your tongue. It is sublime. It is Varasano's.

MAKES 1 (14-INCH) PIZZA, SERVES 3 TO 4

Make the pizza dough at least 2 days ahead. Rest 1 ball of the dough on the counter until it comes to room temperature, about 2 hours. Make the herbed olive oil, adding the minced garlic and the minced basil.

Move an oven rack to the lowest position. Preheat the oven to 500°F for 30 minutes.

Shape the dough and place it on the pizza pan or screen, according to the instructions on page 103. Spread the herbed oil over the dough with a pastry brush, covering the entire surface. Sprinkle with $^1/_4$ cup of the Parmigiano Reggiano. Top with the chopped olives, and cover all with the shredded Emmenthaler.

Bake the pizza for about 15 minutes, until the crust is deep brown and the toppings are bubbling. Check underneath with a metal spatula to ensure the bottom crust is deep brown too. Let the pizza rest for 5 minutes.

Cover the pizza with the arugula. Lay slices of capicola on top. Sprinkle with the remaining $^1/_4$ cup Parmigiano Reggiano and drizzle with the balsamic vinegar. Cut it into 8 wedges and serve.

SALMON DELIGHT

Smoked Salmon ▲ *Cream Cheese* ▲ *Fresh Dill*

Sourdough Pizza Dough (page 102)

1   (8-ounce) tub whipped cream cheese, at room temperature

2   tablespoons chopped fresh dill

1   cup shredded mozzarella

1/2 red onion, peeled and thinly sliced

4   ounces smoked salmon, thinly sliced

3   teaspoons truffle oil

1   tablespoon capers, rinsed

As farmers in Twin Springs Valley, Iowa, Jim and Brenda McCaffrey raised five children, put in huge gardens, and built a pizzeria on their land. The couple went to Rome and Naples to study pizza making, and erected a wood-burning pizza oven. I chose their chic smoked salmon pizza with truffle oil. It's not your usual pizza from a farming family in Iowa! The fresh dill, capers, and truffle oil add subtle depth that brings the pie flavors and textures together.

MAKES 1 (14-INCH) PIZZA, SERVES 3 TO 4

Make the pizza dough at least 2 days ahead. Rest l ball of the dough on the counter until it comes to room temperature, about 2 hours.

Move an oven rack to the lowest position. Preheat the oven to 500˚F for 30 minutes.

Shape the dough and place it on the pizza pan or screen, according to the instructions on page 103. Spread the soft cream cheese over the dough with a rubber spatula, leaving a 1/2-inch border. Sprinkle with l tablespoon of the dill and follow with the shredded mozzarella. Top with the sliced onion. Tear the salmon into small pieces and scatter them over the pizza.

Bake the pizza for about l5 minutes, until the crust is deep brown and the toppings are bubbling. Check underneath with a metal spatula to ensure the bottom crust is deep brown too. Let the pizza rest for 5 minutes.

Brush the rim with l teaspoon of the truffle oil and drizzle the rest over the pizza. Sprinkle with the capers and remaining l tablespoon dill, then cut it into 8 wedges and serve.

PANNA PIZZA

Tomato Sauce ▲ *Cream* ▲ *Fresh Mozzarella*

Sourdough Pizza Dough (page 102)

Cooked Tomato Sauce (page 27)

1 ounce grated Parmigiano Reggiano (1/4 cup)

6 ounces fresh mozzarella

1/2 cup panna or heavy cream

Craig and Annie Stoll beat the odds of opening a successful restaurant in San Francisco. It's difficult to have just one great place, but they have four. They started with a farm-to-table restaurant in 2005. Then they opened a small adjacent space called Pizzeria Delfina, a casual restaurant serving Neapolitan-inspired pies complemented by a changing–daily roster of seasonal antipasti and small entrées.

The Panna Pizza is a simple pleasure with tomato sauce and thick Italian cream called **panna da cucina**. While heavy cream is a fine substitute, if you happen to find **panna** in an Italian specialty store, it makes an extraordinary upgrade.

MAKES 1 (14-INCH) PIZZA, SERVES 2 TO 3

Make the pizza dough at least 2 days ahead. Rest I ball of the dough on the counter until it comes to room temperature, about 2 hours. Make the cooked tomato sauce.

Move an oven rack to the lowest position. Preheat the oven to 500°F for 30 minutes.

Shape the dough and place it on the pizza pan or screen, according to the instructions on page 103. Spread the tomato sauce on the dough with a rubber spatula, leaving a 1/2-inch border. Sprinkle with the Parmigiano Reggiano. Tear the mozzarella into small pieces and scatter them over the pizza. Drizzle with the panna.

Bake the pizza for about 15 minutes, until the crust is deep brown and the toppings are bubbling. Check underneath with a metal spatula to ensure the bottom crust is deep brown too. Let the pizza rest for 5 minutes. Cut it into 8 wedges and serve.

ACAPULCO VERDE PIZZA

Roasted Tomatos ▲ *Black Beans* ▲ *Green Chilis*

**FLYING PIE PIZZA,
BOISE, IDAHO**

Sourdough Pizza
Dough (page 102)

Roasted Tomatoes
(page 31)

**FOR THE BLACK
BEAN SAUCE**

1   tablespoon butter

1/4 cup chopped onion

1   (15-ounce) can
    black beans,
    drained and rinsed

1   cup chicken stock or
    water

2   tablespoons
    balsamic vinegar

1   clove garlic, minced

1/2 cup chopped fresh
    cilantro (from
    about 1/2 bunch)

1   teaspoon salt

1   teaspoon freshly
    ground black
    pepper

1   cup shredded
    mozzarella

4   ounces extra sharp
    cheddar, cut in
    1/2-inch cubes

1/2 cup diced red onion

1   (4-ounce) can diced
    green chiles

Zest and juice of 1 lime

1/4 cup chopped
    scallions

In 1994, this restaurant delivered its one million pie to Sami Babcock, who won pizza for life. That's a pretty great prize, considering Flying Pie has been perfecting its delicious pies since 1978. They are particularly famous for double and triple chile pizzas. Being a green chile lover, the flavor combinations of this pizza called to me. It packs on the spicy flavors of Mexico with roasted green chiles, black beans, and lime.

MAKES 1 (14-INCH) PIZZA, SERVES 3 TO 4

Make the pizza dough at least 2 days ahead. Rest I ball of the dough on the counter until it comes to room temperature, about 2 hours.

Make the roasted tomatoes. Move an oven rack to the lowest position. Increase the oven temperature to 500°F and heat for 15 minutes.

Make the Black Bean Sauce: Melt the butter in a small saucepan over medium heat and sauté the onion for I minute. Add the beans, chicken stock, vinegar, garlic, 1/4 cup of the cilantro, the salt, and the pepper. Cook to reduce the liquid by half, about 15 minutes. Remove the bean sauce from the heat. Stir in the remaining 1/4 cup cilantro.

Shape the dough and place it on the pizza pan or screen, according to the instructions on page 103. Spread the bean sauce on the pizza with a rubber spatula, leaving a I-inch border. Sprinkle the mozzarella on top, followed by the cheddar and red onion. Scatter the roasted tomato wedges on top. Mix the chiles with the lime zest and juice in a small bowl and place small spoonfuls around the pizza.

Bake the pizza for about 20 minutes, until the crust is deep brown and the toppings are bubbling. Check underneath with a metal spatula to ensure the bottom is deep brown. Let the pizza rest for 5 minutes. Sprinkle with the chopped scallions, then cut it into 8 wedges and serve.

ROSA PIZZA

Pistachios ▲ Rosemary ▲ Red Onion

Sourdough Pizza Dough (page 102)

Herbed Olive Oil (page 31)

1 ounce grated Parmigiano Reggiano (¹/4 cup)

³/4 cup chopped salted pistachios

2 tablespoons coarsely chopped fresh rosemary

¹/2 red onion, peeled and thinly sliced

8 ounces fresh mozzarella

In 1988, a young pizzaiolo got permission to work in a neighborhood grocery store on a dusty road in Arizona, and make pizza. Thus began an artisan food movement that defines the essence of good food. You see, it's not just any pizza. Chris Bianco decides what he puts on that pizza based on ingredients from local farmers.

Today, he is now known from coast to coast as a visionary pizza maker. Here is my humble interpretation of his Rosa Pizza. This pizza personifies the dry desert, with its piney rosemary and toasty, earthy pistachios. These unusual pizza flavorings come together in an artful way.

MAKES 1 (14-INCH) PIZZA, SERVES 3 TO 4

Make the pizza dough at least 2 days ahead. Rest I ball of the dough on the counter until it comes to room temperature, about 2 hours. Make the herbed olive oil.

Move an oven rack to the lowest position. Preheat the oven to 500°F for 30 minutes.

Shape the dough and place it on the pizza pan or screen, according to the instructions on page 103. Spread half the herbed oil over the dough with a pastry brush, covering the entire surface. Sprinkle with the Parmigiano Reggiano, pistachios, and rosemary and top with the onion slices. Break the mozzarella into small pieces and scatter them over the pizza. Drizzle the remaining herbed oil on top.

Bake the pizza for about I5 minutes, until the crust is deep brown and the toppings are bubbling. Check underneath with a metal spatula to ensure the bottom crust is deep brown too. Let the pizza rest for 5 minutes. Cut it into 8 wedges and serve.

PIZZA FIORE

Squash Blossoms ▲ Tomato Sauce ▲ Burrata

Sourdough Pizza Dough (page 102)

Cooked Tomato Sauce (page 27)

16 fresh squash blossoms

1 ounce grated Parmigiano Reggiano ($^1/_4$ cup)

8 ounces burrata cheese, drained

2 tablespoons extra-virgin olive oil

When Mario Batali, Joe Bastianich, and Nancy Silverton opened this restaurant, these superstars of hospitality made casual pizza an upscale event. Mozza is a small place that's hot and hip. Reservations are hard to get and lines often stretch down the street.

I love this simple Pizza Fiore, with creamy burrata that is milky and luscious. Delicate squash blossoms make it an Italian rite of summer. Head to the farmers' market to find these pretty yellow flowers that taste faintly of zucchini, but sweeter. If they're not in season, you could still top the pizza with the Roasted Zucchini (page 34), which adds a caramel flavor.

MAKES 1 (14-INCH) PIZZA, SERVES 3 TO 4

Make the pizza dough at least 2 days ahead. Rest I ball of the dough on the counter until it comes to room temperature, about 2 hours. Make the tomato sauce.

Move an oven rack to the lowest position. Preheat the oven to 500˚F for 30 minutes.

Snap off the stems of the zucchini flowers. Do not wash them. Check inside the flowers to make sure there are no insects.

Shape the dough and place it on the pizza pan or screen, according to the instructions on page 103. Spread the sauce on the pizza with a rubber spatula, leaving a I-inch border. Sprinkle with Parmigiano Reggiano. Tear off teaspoonfuls of the burrata and place them on top. Place the squash blossoms around the pizza in a circular pattern. Drizzle the pizza with the olive oil.

Bake the pizza for I5 to 20 minutes, until the crust is deep brown and the toppings are bubbling. Check underneath with a metal spatula to ensure the bottom crust is deep brown too. Let the pizza rest for 5 minutes. Cut it into 8 wedges and serve.

Chapter 7

STUFFED PIZZAS

Millions of Americans, mostly across the Midwest and East Coast, consume stuffed pizzas, chowing down on thick pies filled with well-seasoned beef or sausage and gooey cheese.

There's something dramatic and beautiful when one of these big, homey pizzas comes out of the oven. They are not the usual thin pizza rounds with sauce, but half-moons, torpedoes, and double-crust pies that are golden brown and crispy, with the promise of a luscious filling within.

Yes, these pies are a little retro, but once you taste them you will realize that you have missed this combination of meat and cheese, and you would like to eat it more often. It's fun to eat pizza that's more like a sandwich, with crispy dough on both sides of the filling. Leftovers—if there are any—crisp up beautifully in the oven the next day, and stuffed pizzas also taste great cold.

Most of these stuffed pizzas are Italian in flavor and ingredients, probably because the inventors of stuffed pies, who came from two Chicago chains in the mid-1970s, were Italian. They said they based their recipes on Easter pies, called *scarciedda,* made by their families in Turin, Italy. Perhaps they were inspired by the success of the deep-dish pie. The classic deep dish has a crust about 3 inches high, and lots of cheese, meat, and sauce that requires longer baking. Some pizzerias have experimented with the stuffed pizza form and created something entirely new, like Dove Vivi's Deep-Dish Reuben Pizza. That combination of beef, sauerkraut, cheese, and dressing will haunt you.

STUFFED CRUST DOUGH

1³/₄ cups unbleached all-purpose flour, plus more for dusting

³/₄ cup warm water

3 tablespoons cornmeal

2 tablespoons extra-virgin olive oil, plus more for the bowl

1 teaspoon active dry yeast

¹/₂ teaspoon salt

Nonstick cooking spray

This durable dough is easy to handle, which is useful because some recipes require you to fold it or turn it into shapes. You may also need to double this recipe, if you're making a pie with a double crust. You'll be rewarded with a rich dough that is full of flavor, and which cooks to a crispy golden brown.

Make this dough up to three days or seventy-two hours in advance. Do not let it sit out for more than one hour because it gets too soft and will be difficult to shape.

MAKES 1 (12- OR 14-INCH) PIZZA CRUST

Place the flour, water, cornmeal, oil, and yeast in the bowl of a stand mixer fitted with the dough hook. Mix on low to combine, about 2 minutes.

Turn off the mixer and let the dough rest for about 10 minutes. Add the salt, then knead the dough on medium speed for about 8 minutes, until it is firm, smooth, and supple. If the dough seems too dry, add 1 or 2 teaspoons water.

Pour 1 teaspoon of olive oil into a medium bowl. Shape the dough into a ball and place it in the bowl. Turn the dough to coat it with the oil. This prevents a crust from forming on its surface as it rises. Cover the bowl with plastic wrap and let the dough rise in the refrigerator overnight or for at least 12 hours. The dough will double in volume. Rest the dough on the counter until it comes to room temperature, about 1 hour. Do not let it sit on the counter longer, as it becomes too soft.

Get the Dough in Shape

STRETCH THE DOUGH Lightly flour a clean, dry countertop. Gently place the round of dough on your counter. Do not knead or press on it. Instead, let it settle. Dust the top with flour.

With your fingertips, press in the center of the ball lightly with one hand, while rotating the ball with the other hand and pulling the dough outward into a circle. Add more flour, if necessary, to ensure the dough slides easily. Slide your hands under the dough and pick it up. Let the dough fall around your hands to stretch it. A 1-inch rim

should occur naturally. The dough should be 14 inches in diameter.

PLACE THE DOUGH ON THE PAN OR SCREEN If the stuffed pizza recipe calls for a pan, spray a 14-inch pan with the nonstick cooking spray and place it next to the shaped dough. Quickly pick up the shaped dough while sliding it onto the pan. Reshape as necessary to fit the pan. If making a deep-dish pie, you'll find instructions in the recipe. Your stuffed crust dough is now ready for the fillings.

THE GOODIE ROONIE

Sausage ▲ Tomato Sauce ▲ Mozzarella

Stuffed Crust Dough
(page 123), doubled

Chunky Tomato Sauce
(page 27)

1 pound mild Italian
sausage meat

1 ounce grated
Parmigiano
Reggiano (¹/₄ cup)

2 cups shredded
mozzarella

¹/₂ white onion, peeled
and thinly sliced

Families pile into Big Fred's restaurant to watch college basketball and eat exceptional pizza. The Cornhuskers have two official mascots, who keep the crowd roaring through the games. Big Fred's has an unofficial mascot: the Goodie Roonie. The restaurant advertises the pie in its own box on the menu because it's so good it deserves stand-alone status.

A double-crust pizza filled with gooey cheese and ground beef or sausage (I prefer the sausage), it looks dramatic on your dining room table, like a crusty golden UFO. Your guests will *ooh* and *ahh* when you cut in and serve a slice. You can eat it like a sandwich, so bake it and take it to a game—it'll get you revved up to root for your team.

MAKES 1 (14-INCH) DOUBLE-CRUST PIZZA, SERVES 4

Make a double dough recipe at least 12 hours ahead. Rest the dough on the counter until it comes to room temperature, no more than 1 hour. Make the chunky tomato sauce at least 1 hour ahead.

Move an oven rack to the lowest position. Preheat the oven to 500°F for 30 minutes.

Cook the sausage in a medium skillet over medium-high heat, breaking it up with a spoon. Brown until all the sausage is fully cooked and crumbly, about 15 minutes. Use a slotted spoon to transfer the sausage to a bowl lined with paper towels.

Shape half the dough and place it on the pizza pan or screen, according to the instructions on page 123. Spread the tomato sauce on the dough with a rubber spatula, leaving a 1-inch border. Sprinkle with the Parmigiano Reggiano, followed by the mozzarella, sausage, and onion.

Form another 14-inch round with the other half of the dough. Lay this round of dough on top of the pizza and pinch the edges of both doughs together to seal them. Push the dough edges together, pressing hard with your fingers until you almost pinch through the dough. Then fold the edge over into a seam. Press it down tightly to prevent leaks.

Bake the pizza for about 20 minutes, or until the top and bottom crusts are deep brown. Let the pizza rest for 5 minutes. Cut it into 8 wedges and serve.

DEEP-DISH REUBEN PIZZA WITH ZUCCHINI PICKLE RELISH

Corned Beef ▲ *Swiss Cheese* ▲ *Sauerkraut*

Stuffed Crust Dough (page 123), doubled

FOR THE ZUCCHINI PICKLE RELISH

1 medium green zucchini, diced

1 medium yellow squash, diced

1 medium red onion, peeled and diced

2 tablespoons salt

1 1/2 cups sugar

1 cup white vinegar

1 tablespoon cornstarch

1 teaspoon ground turmeric

1 teaspoon celery seed

1 teaspoon mustard seed

Nonstick cooking spray

12 ounces Swiss cheese, cut into 1/2-inch cubes (about 2 cups)

1 1/2 pounds thinly sliced cooked corned beef or pastrami

1 (14-ounce) jar sauerkraut, drained (about 2 cups)

1/2 cup chili sauce

1/2 cup mayonnaise

1 teaspoon cornstarch

DOVE VIVI, PORTLAND, OREGON

A Reuben pizza sounds strange, but this deep-dish pie was so good I couldn't stop eating it. It's tangy, crispy, salty, and creamy all at once. If you love Reuben sandwiches, you won't believe how delicious it is. It's a double-crust pizza, but more like an enormous crispy bread stuffed with goodies.

This pizza was a special on the day I visited, and the zucchini relish is my addition. I based it on an old-fashioned sweet pickle still sold in stores in the South. Salting the zucchini and onion helps crisp and condense them so the relish doesn't get mushy.

MAKES 1 (14-INCH) DEEP-DISH PIZZA, SERVES 8

Make a double dough recipe at least 12 hours ahead. Rest the dough on the counter until it comes to room temperature, no more than 1 hour.

Make the Zucchini Relish: Place the zucchini, squash, and onion in a colander set in the sink and add the salt. Stir thoroughly. Let the vegetables sit for about an hour or up to overnight. Rinse off the salt and drain.

Move an oven rack to the lowest position. Preheat the oven to 375°F.

Combine the sugar, vinegar, cornstarch, turmeric, and celery and mustard seeds in a medium skillet over medium-high heat. Stir until the sugar melts. Throw in the zucchini, squash, and onion and stir. Cook until thick and shiny, and some of the liquid has evaporated, about 10 minutes. Transfer to a bowl and refrigerate until cold.

(continued)

Spray a 14 x 2-inch deep-dish pizza pan with nonstick cooking spray. Shape half the dough according to the instructions on page 123. Make the round of dough about 1 inch larger than the bottom of the pan. Press the dough into the pan, covering the bottom and sides. Keep the thickness even.

Toss $1/2$ cup of the cheese cubes on the bottom of the crust. Add the corned beef, then the remaining cheese, and the sauerkraut in two layers. Mix the chili sauce, mayonnaise, and cornstarch in a small bowl and pour it over the pizza.

Form another 14-inch round with the other half of the dough. Lay this round of dough on top of the pizza and pinch the edges of both doughs together to seal them. Push the dough edges together, pressing hard with your fingers until you almost pinch through the dough. Then fold the edge over into a seam. Press it down tightly to prevent leaks.

Bake for about 1 hour, until the crust is brown and the inside is bubbling through the crust. Let the pizza rest for 5 minutes. Cut it into 8 slices and serve with a spoonful of relish.

STEAK STROMBOLI

Steak ▲ Mozzarella ▲ Tomato Dipping Sauce

Stuffed Crust Dough (page 123)

FOR THE ROASTED STEAK

1 pound round steak or top sirloin, sliced paper thin

2 cubes beef bouillon

6 cloves garlic, minced

1/2 onion, peeled and thinly sliced

1 teaspoon dried oregano

1/2 teaspoon freshly ground black pepper

Cooked Tomato Sauce (page 27)

1 cup shredded mozzarella

Nonstick cooking spray

1 tablespoon extra-virgin olive oil

1 ounce grated Parmigiano Reggiano (1/4 cup)

In 1920, Nat Romano left an Italy run by the harsh dictatorship of Mussolini and settled in Essington, Pennsylvania. Times were hard but Nat started a storefront business selling tomato pies the way he had made them in Italy. One day, Nat created a baked sandwich, stuffing sandwich fixings inside the dough. When these new creations came out of the oven, customers dove into them, excited by turnover-like pizzas shaped like a torpedo. A close friend, inspired by the 1950 movie *Stromboli,* with Ingrid Bergman, suggested that he call his new creation the stromboli. That's how Nat's pizza became known throughout the world.

This meaty pizza is filled with juicy steak strips that are braised for 1 1/2 hours until tender, and topped with oozing mozzarella. Serve tomato sauce on the side for dipping.

MAKES 1 (12-INCH) STROMBOLI, SERVES 2 GENEROUSLY

Make the dough up to 12 hours ahead.

Make the Roasted Steak: Preheat the oven to 400°F. Place the steak slices, bouillon, garlic, onion, oregano, and pepper in a small Dutch oven or roasting pan with 2 cups water. Stir together and roast, uncovered, for 1 1/2 hours, until the meat is browned and tender and the juices have evaporated. Check the meat a few times. If it is drying out, add 1/4 cup water. The meat will be tender and browned when ready. Let the meat cool for 15 minutes and, if any liquid remains, drain when ready to use. Keep the oven on.

While the meat cooks, make the cooked tomato sauce. Rest the dough on the counter until it comes to room temperature, no more than 1 hour.

Move an oven rack to the lowest position. Increase the oven temperature to 500°F and heat for 15 minutes.

Shape the dough into a 12-inch round, according to the instructions on page 123. Spoon 2 tablespoons of the tomato sauce onto the middle of the dough and spread it out with a rubber spatula. Sprinkle the mozzarella on the tomato sauce. Top with the sliced steak.

Fold the pizza in half by bringing the dough over the filling in a half-moon shape. Push the dough edges together, pressing hard with your fingers until you almost pinch through the dough. Then fold the edge over into a seam. Press it down tightly to prevent leaks. Roll the stromboli over, so the seam is underneath. Tuck the ends under to form a torpedo shape, like a football. Spray a 14-inch pan or screen with nonstick cooking spray. Transfer the stromboli to the pan.

Bake the stromboli for about 15 minutes, until the crust is deep brown. Remove from the oven and brush the crust with a little olive oil. Sprinkle with the Parmigiano Reggiano. Let the stomboli rest for 5 minutes. Cut the stromboli in half lengthwise and widthwise so you have 4 equal pieces. Serve with the remaining tomato sauce on the side.

NIC-O-BOLI

Ground Beef ▲ Tomato Sauce ▲ Mozzarella

Stuffed Crust Dough
   (page 123)

Cooked Tomato Sauce
   (page 27)

1   pound ground beef

1/2 teaspoon salt

1/2 teaspoon pepper

2   cups shredded
      mozzarella

Nonstick cooking spray

1   tablespoon extra-
      virgin olive oil

NICOLA PIZZA,
REHOBOTH, DELAWARE

Nicholas Caggiano claims that he invented the Nic-O-Boli. It makes sense, since it's his name and the word *stromboli* combined. Caggiano now makes over seventeen varieties of Nic-O-Bolis at Nicola Pizza and ships them all over the world.

   One of my favorites is a simple pie filled with ground beef, mozzarella, and tomato sauce. Make this at home, and if you like it, give Nick a call and order a case to enjoy throughout the year.

MAKES 1 (12-INCH) STROMBOLI, SERVES 2 GENEROUSLY

Make the dough at least 12 hours ahead. Rest the dough on the counter until it comes to room temperature, no more than 1 hour. Make the cooked tomato sauce.

Move an oven rack to the lowest position. Preheat the oven to 500°F for 30 minutes.

Heat a medium skillet over medium-high heat. Add the ground beef, breaking it up with a spoon. Add the salt and pepper and stir. Cook until the beef is fully cooked and crispy on the edges, about 10 minutes. Use a slotted spoon to transfer the beef to a bowl lined with paper towels.

Shape the dough into a 12-inch round, according to the instructions on page 123. Spread the tomato sauce onto half of the dough with a rubber spatula, leaving a 1-inch rim. Cover the sauce with the ground beef and top with the shredded mozzarella.

Fold the pizza in half by bringing the dough over the filling in a half-moon shape. Push the dough edges together with your fingers, pressing hard until you almost pinch through the dough. Then fold the edge over into a seam. Press it down tightly to prevent leaks. Roll the stromboli over until the seam is underneath. Tuck the ends under to form a torpedo shape, like a football. Spray a 14-inch pan or screen with nonstick cooking spray. Transfer the stromboli to the pan.

Bake the stromboli for about 15 minutes, until the crust is deep brown. Remove from the oven and brush the crust with the olive oil. Let the stromboli rest for 5 minutes. Cut the stromboli in half lengthwise and widthwise into 4 equal pieces and serve.

ORIGINAL DEEP DISH

Sausage ▲ Pepperoni ▲ Green Peppers

Stuffed Crust Dough (page 123)

Chunky Tomato Sauce (page 27)

Nonstick cooking spray

2   tablespoons cornmeal

8   ounces mild Italian sausage meat

12 ounces fresh mozzarella, sliced

1/2 cup sliced fresh mushrooms

1/4 cup diced onion

2   ounces pepperoni slices

1/4 cup diced green bell pepper

1   ounce grated Parmigiano Reggiano (1/4 cup)

UNO PIZZERIA & GRILL, CHICAGO, ILLINOIS

In 1943, Ike Sewell opened a new type of restaurant at the corner of Ohio and Wabash in Chicago. Nobody had ever seen pizza like this before. Ike loaded a deep pie pan with dough, sausage, and cheese, and put tomato sauce on top. He baked it for almost an hour and served the 2-inch-high pizza piping hot. One slice is plenty for a meal.

Pizzeria Uno served the first deep-dish pizza in the United States. Through the years this restaurant has always strived to be the best. Uno is an appropriate name for this iconic place.

MAKES 1 (12-INCH) DEEP-DISH PIZZA, SERVES 4

Make the dough I day ahead. Rest the dough on the counter until it comes to room temperature, no more than I hour. Make the chunky tomato sauce I hour ahead.

Move an oven rack to the lowest position. Preheat the oven to 500°F for 30 minutes.

Spray a 12 x 2-inch deep-dish pizza pan with nonstick cooking spray. Shape the dough according to the instructions on page 123. Make the round of dough about I inch larger than the bottom of the pan. Press the dough into the pan, covering the bottom and sides. Keep the thickness even.

Press the raw sausage into the bottom dough evenly. Layer the mozzarella over the top, followed by the mushrooms, onion, pepperoni, and bell pepper. Pour the sauce over all and sprinkle with the Parmigiano Reggiano.

Bake the pizza for about 45 minutes, until the crust is a deep brown and the fillings are bubbly. Let the pizza rest for about 5 minutes. Cut it into 8 wedges and serve.

PIEROGI PIZZA

Mashed Potato ▲ Havarti ▲ Sour Cream

Stuffed Crust Dough
(page 123)

2 pounds Russet
potatoes, peeled
and cut into 1-inch
pieces

2 tablespoons plus
2 teaspoons salt

1 (8-ounce) container
sour cream

2 tablespoons butter

1/2 cup half-and-half

1 tablespoon chopped
fresh flat-leaf
parsley

9 ounces Havarti, cut
into 1/2-inch cubes
(2 cups)

All-purpose flour, for
dusting

Nonstick cooking spray

1 tablespoon extra-
virgin olive oil

Ever hear of Old Forge–style pizza? Unless you're from somewhere near the town in Pennsylvania, you probably have not. This cheesy mashed potato pie is served almost exclusively within a fifteen-mile radius of Old Forge, in taverns and specialty restaurants. Some of these places have been making this type of pie for more than seventy years. Coal miners were among the first to enjoy it. They came into the restaurants to eat and play cards.

Old Forge pizza comes in two varieties, red and white. The red variety is similar to Sicilian-style pizza but softer and saucier, filled with creamy cheese such as white American or fontina. I like this white Pierogi Pizza. It's like eating a crispy mashed potato and cheese sandwich. Here is comfort food at its finest. Serve it as a side dish, with a salad and grilled sausages.

MAKES 1 STUFFED (12 X 10-INCH) PIZZA, SERVES 4 GENEROUSLY

Make the dough at least 12 hours ahead. Rest the dough on the counter until it comes to room temperature, no more than 1 hour.

Move an oven rack to the lowest position. Preheat the oven to 500°F for 30 minutes.

Tip the potatoes into a large pot, cover them with water, and add 2 tablespoons of the salt. Bring the water to a boil over high heat and boil for about 10 minutes, until the potatoes are soft. Drain the potatoes in a colander set in the sink and return them to the pot. Add the sour cream, butter, half-and-half, the remaining 2 teaspoons salt, and the parsley. Use a potato masher or a thick wire whisk to mash the potatoes until soft and creamy.

Lightly flour a clean, dry countertop. Shape the dough into a 12 x 18-inch rectangle. Cover half of the dough with 1 cup of the cubed cheese, leaving a 1-inch rim. Mound the mashed potato filling over the cheese and then mound the remaining cheese over the potatoes.

Fold the other half of the dough over the filling. It might look like too much filling, but it will fit. Press the dough edges together, pushing down hard with your fingers until you almost pinch through the dough. Then fold the pinched edge over into a seam. Press it down tightly to prevent leaks. It will look like a 12 x 10-inch rectangle crimped on three sides. Spray a 14-inch pan or screen with nonstick cooking spray. Transfer the pie to the pan.

Bake for about 15 minutes, until the crust is deep brown. Remove from the oven and brush the crust with the olive oil. Let it rest for 5 minutes. Give it a quick whack with a big knife and it will cut easily. If you saw back and forth, the potato will ooze out. Cut it into 8 pieces and serve.

THE ARTIE STUFFY

Marinated Artichokes ▲ *Tomato Sauce* ▲ *Mushrooms*

Stuffed Crust Dough (page 123), doubled

Cooked Tomato Sauce (page 27), doubled

8 ounces fresh mozzarella

4 (6.5-ounce) jars marinated artichoke hearts, drained

1 cup sliced fresh mushrooms

2 cups shredded mozzarella

1 ounce grated Parmigiano Reggiano (1/4 cup)

Stuffed-crust pizzas are the claim to fame at Damgoode Pies. The Artie Stuffy caught my eye because I liked the name, and I like artichokes too. Too few pizzas feature them, particularly in this quantity. In this double-crust pizza, you'll find creamy, stretchy cheese layered between plump tomato bits and tangy marinated artichokes. It's damn good, if you ask me.

MAKES 1 (14-INCH) PIZZA, SERVES 8

Make a double dough recipe I day ahead. Rest the dough on the counter until it comes to room temperature, no more than I hour. Make the cooked tomato sauce.

Move an oven rack to the lowest position. Preheat the oven to 500°F for 30 minutes.

Shape half the dough and place it on the pizza pan or screen, according to the instructions on page 123. Spread half of the tomato sauce on the dough with a rubber spatula, leaving a I-inch rim. Tear the fresh mozzarella into small pieces and scatter them over the sauce. Top with the artichoke pieces and mushrooms. Sprinkle with the shredded mozzarella.

Form a 14-inch round with the other half of the dough. Lay this round of dough on top of the pizza and pinch the edges of both doughs together to seal them. Push the dough edges together, pressing hard with your fingers until you almost pinch through the dough. Then fold the edge over into a seam. Press it down tightly to prevent leaks. Spread the remaining tomato sauce over the top crust with a rubber spatula, up to the outer rim. Sprinkle the Parmigiano Reggiano on top of the sauce.

Bake for about 20 minutes, or until the top and bottom crusts are deep brown. Let the pizza rest for 5 minutes. Cut it into 8 slices and serve.

Chapter 8

CORN FLOUR PIZZAS

You've heard of cornmeal pizzas, but corn flour? Yes, definitely. It's an improvement. Corn flour creates a light, delicate crust compared to cornmeal, which can get heavy. It's also a nice change from a white flour crust, which sometimes includes a bit of cornmeal for texture and crunch. Because the dough is light and crisp, with no oil, the pizzas are not heavy at all. This soft corn flour crust browns easily, so be sure to watch the pizza toward the end.

Some of the pizzas in this chapter are deep dish. You'll also find the classic combination of cornbread and beans in the Latin Lover, and a modern pairing of chicken breast with mandarin oranges. Rustica in Oakland, California, adds fennel seed to the crust for a little more flavor. So take a look at all the pizzas you can make with a corn flour crust, whip up some dough, and give them a try.

CORN FLOUR PIZZA DOUGH

1¼ cups unbleached all-purpose flour, plus more for dusting

½ cup corn flour

1 teaspoon active dry yeast

1 tablespoon sugar

½ cup plus 2 tablespoons water

1 teaspoon salt

1 teaspoon olive oil

Nonstick cooking spray

Corn flour is just finely ground cornmeal. I found a bag of Bob's Red Mill corn flour in my grocery store. You can use cornmeal but it won't be as light and golden as the corn flour. To make your own corn flour, grind a scant ½ cup cornmeal in a blender and then measure the amount again to get a full ½ cup corn flour—the amount you'll need to make the dough.

Make this dough at least twelve and up to seventy-two hours ahead. Let it come to room temperature for about one hour before using.

MAKES ENOUGH DOUGH FOR 1 (12-INCH) PIZZA CRUST

Place the flours, yeast, sugar, and water in the bowl of a stand mixer fitted with the dough hook. Mix on low to combine, about 2 minutes.

Turn off the mixer and let the dough rest for about 10 minutes. Add the salt, then knead the dough on medium speed for about 5 minutes, until the dough is firm, smooth, and supple. If the dough seems too dry, add more water, a few drops at a time.

Pour the olive oil into a medium bowl. Shape the dough into a ball and place it in the bowl. Turn the dough to coat it with the oil. This prevents a crust from forming on its surface as it rises. Cover the bowl with plastic wrap and let the dough rise in the refrigerator. After about 12 hours, the dough will double in volume. Rest the dough on the counter until it comes to room temperature, about 1 hour.

Get the Dough in Shape

STRETCH THE DOUGH FOR A PIZZA PAN OR SCREEN Lightly flour a clean, dry countertop. Gently place the round of dough on your counter. Do not knead or press on it. Instead, let it settle. Dust the top with flour.

Make dimples in the dough with your fingertips by pressing down in the middle to stretch it out. Move the dough around in a circle as you press down with your fingertips. A 1-inch rim should occur naturally. Press your fingertips along the inside of the rim, moving in a circle. Place your hands on the dough, fingers up against the rim, and push out while turning in a circle. Add more flour, if necessary, to ensure the dough slides easily.

Finish stretching the dough by sliding your hands underneath it and picking it up. Let the dough fall around your hands to stretch it. Keep your hands along the edges, rather than in the middle. The dough should be 12 inches in diameter.

PLACE THE DOUGH ON THE PAN OR SCREEN Spray a 14-inch pizza pan with nonstick cooking spray and place it next to the shaped dough. Quickly pick up the shaped dough while sliding it onto the pan. Reshape as necessary.

STRETCH THE DOUGH FOR A DEEP-DISH PIZZA PAN Lightly flour a clean, dry countertop. Gently place the round of dough on your counter. Do not knead or press on it. Instead, let it settle. With your fingertips, press into the center of the ball lightly with one hand, while rotating the ball with the other hand and pulling the dough outward into a circle. Slide your hands under the dough and pick it up. Let the dough fall around your hands to stretch it. Make a round of dough that is at least 1 inch larger than the pan. (You can also roll out the dough.)

Transfer the dough to the pan and press it in evenly. Build a wall of crust about 1½ inches up the side of the pan. Keep the thickness even. Your corn flour dough is now ready for the pizza toppings.

THE FLYING PIGGIE PIZZA

Pulled Pork ▲ *Onion Straws* ▲ *Barbecue Sauce*

Corn Flour Pizza Dough (page 140)

FOR THE PULLED PORK

1   pound boneless pork, from the shoulder, blade, or butt; or boneless ribs

2   cloves garlic, chopped

1   tablespoon liquid smoke

1   teaspoon salt

1   teaspoon freshly ground black pepper

1   cup barbecue sauce

FOR THE FRIED ONION STRAWS

1   large white onion, peeled, quartered, and thinly sliced

1¹/₂ cups buttermilk

1¹/₂ cups all-purpose flour

¹/₂ teaspoon garlic powder

¹/₂ teaspoon cayenne pepper

1   teaspoon salt

2   cups shredded mozzarella

¹/₂ cup bread and butter pickles or dill pickles, sliced into thin strips

¹/₂ cup canola oil

Salt

The year was 1980. The scene was Las Vegas, a hotbed for moneymakers, and movers and shakers. Casinos were going up like gangbusters and the scent of money was in the air. The scent of pizza was there too. Two cousins, Sam and John, saw an opportunity all the way from New York. They borrowed a car and hopped across the United States to open Metro Pizza in the heart of Vegas. When they arrived, they had nothing but two ovens and a cash register.

After thirty years, the same two cousins can be found in their pizza shop with the two original ovens and lots of pizzas baking in them. The Flying Piggie is their pulled pork pizza, and it tastes like Southern barbecue with a scattering of onion straws on top. This pizza uses prepared barbecue sauce. I like Open Pit because it is vinegary, and not too thick or sweet. If your barbecue sauce is sweet, use dill chips instead of bread and butter pickles.

The pork takes about two hours to cook. Pan-fry the onions just before the pizza comes out of the oven, to make sure they're crisp and hot when the pizza is ready to eat.

MAKES 1 (12-INCH) PIZZA, SERVES 2 TO 3

Make the pizza dough at least 12 hours ahead. Rest the dough on the counter until it comes to room temperature, about 1 hour.

Make the Pulled Pork: Preheat the oven to 400°F. Place the pork in a small roasting pan or Dutch oven with 2 cups water, the garlic, liquid smoke, salt, and pepper. It's fine if the meat is not completely submerged. Cover the pan with foil and roast for about 2 hours, until the pork is soft and tender and pulls apart easily with a fork. Let

cool, then transfer the pork to a cutting board and shred with two forks. Transfer the meat to a medium bowl, add the barbecue sauce, and mix thoroughly. Keep the oven on.

Meanwhile, make the Fried Onion Straws: Place the onion slices in a medium bowl and pour the buttermilk over them to coat. Soak the onion for 1 hour. In another large bowl, mix the flour, garlic, cayenne, and salt.

Rest the dough on the counter until it comes to room temperature, about 1 hour. Move an oven rack to the lowest position. Increase the oven temperature to 500°F. Heat for 15 minutes.

Shape the dough and place it on the pizza pan or screen, according to the instructions on page 141. Sprinkle with the mozzarella, leaving a 1-inch border. Drop spoonfuls of the pork on top, followed by the pickle strips.

Bake the pizza for about 13 minutes, until the crust is deep brown and the toppings are bubbling. Check underneath with a metal spatula to ensure the bottom crust is deep brown too. Let the pizza rest for 5 minutes.

Fry the onion when the pizza has 5 minutes left to bake. Drain the onion, shaking off excess buttermilk, and toss the slices into the spiced flour until well coated. Heat $1/4$ cup of the canola oil in a medium skillet over medium-high heat. Pan-fry the onions in two batches, stirring continuously and cooking until brown and crispy, about 3 minutes. Add the remaining $1/4$ cup canola oil to the pan and cook the second batch. Transfer the fried onion to paper towels and sprinkle with salt.

Top the pizza with the crispy onion, spreading it out across the pie in stacks. Cut the pizza into 8 wedges and serve.

CHICAGO FIRE PIZZA

Sausage ▲ Roasted Red Peppers ▲ Jalapeño

Corn Flour Pizza Dough (page 140)

Chunky Tomato Sauce (page 27)

Roasted Red Pepper Strips (page 32)

1 jalapeño pepper, seeded and halved

1 teaspoon extra-virgin olive oil

Nonstick cooking spray

2 tablespoons cornmeal

12 ounces hot Italian sausage meat

16 ounces fresh mozzarella, sliced into $1/2$-inch-thick rounds

$1/2$ cup sliced red onion

1 ounce grated Parmigiano Reggiano ($1/4$ cup)

GINO'S EAST, CHICAGO, ILLINOIS

In the 1960s, two cab drivers complained to each other every day that the Chicago traffic was really bad. They wanted to remove themselves from the daily grind of the downtown loop. They had a plan: If they couldn't stop the traffic, they could at least benefit from it. So in 1966, they opened Gino's East Pizzeria on Superior Street, in the heart of all that bad traffic.

That was genius, and so are their pizzas. These are true Chicago deep-dish pies with crunchy, chewy, corn flour crusts. I like their spicy version, the Chicago Fire, with sausage, roasted peppers, and jalapeños. It doesn't get any hotter than this, and the traffic's still bad here in Chicago!

MAKES 1 (12-INCH) PIZZA, SERVES 2 TO 3

Make the pizza dough at least 12 hours ahead. Rest the dough on the counter until it comes to room temperature, about 1 hour. Make the chunky tomato sauce 1 hour ahead. Make the roasted red pepper strips.

Preheat the oven to 500°F for 30 minutes.

Place the jalapeño halves on a small sheet pan coated with the olive oil. Roast for 15 minutes, then let cool and thinly slice. Keep the oven on and move an oven rack to the lowest position.

Spray a 12 x 2-inch deep-dish pizza pan with nonstick cooking spray. Sprinkle with the cornmeal.

Shape the dough for a deep-dish pizza pan, according to the instructions on page 141. Press the uncooked sausage evenly into the bottom, and add the mozzarella. Sprinkle with the onion, roasted red pepper, and jalapeño. Pour the tomato sauce over the pizza and sprinkle with the Parmigiano Reggiano.

Bake the pizza for about 30 minutes, until the crust is deep brown and the toppings are bubbling. Check underneath with a metal spatula to ensure the bottom crust is deep brown too. Let the pizza rest for 5 minutes. Cut it into 8 slices and serve.

LATIN LOVER PIZZA

Sausage ▲ *Refried Beans* ▲ *Jalapeño*

Corn Flour Pizza
Dough (page 140)

1 tablespoon extra-
virgin olive oil

2 tablespoons minced
onion

1 clove garlic, minced

1 (16-ounce) can pinto
beans, drained

12 ounces linguiça or
Andouille sausage,
halved lengthwise
and sliced into half-
moons

1 cup shredded
mozzarella

1 cup shredded sharp
cheddar

12 cherry tomatoes,
halved

1 jalapeño pepper,
seeded and thinly
sliced

2 tablespoons
chopped fresh
cilantro

PIZZA ORGASMICA,
SAN FRANCISCO,
CALIFORNIA

With pizza names such as Ménage à Trois and Doggie Style, it's easy to guess what these guys focus on. I see their point. Why not describe pizza as sensual and alluring? Eating pizza sets off pleasure centers in your brain, sending dopamine and other hormones racing through your endocrine system.

Pizza Orgasmica knows this, and the Latin Lover Pizza was love at first sight. Spicy Portuguese sausage and oniony refried beans mingle on a crispy corn crust. The hot bubbly cheddar on top seals the deal for a happy ending.

MAKES 1 (12-INCH) PIZZA, SERVES 2 TO 3

Make the pizza dough at least 12 hours ahead. Rest the dough on the counter until it comes to room temperature, about 1 hour.

Move an oven rack to the lowest position. Preheat the oven to 500°F for 30 minutes.

Heat the olive oil in a medium skillet over medium-high heat. Add the onion and garlic and sauté for 1 minute. Add the pinto beans and 1 cup water. Crush the pinto beans with a potato masher or a big spoon. Cook, stirring occasionally, until the mashed beans soak up the water and thicken into a paste, about 10 minutes. Turn off the heat.

In a medium skillet over medium-high heat, cook the sausage until brown and crispy, stirring occasionally, about 5 minutes. Using a slotted spoon, transfer the sausage to paper towels.

Shape the dough and place it on the pizza pan or screen, according to the instructions on page 141. Spread the beans over the dough with a rubber spatula. Sprinkle with the mozzarella and then the cheddar. Top with the sausage, cherry tomatoes, and jalapeño.

Bake the pizza for about 15 minutes, until the crust is deep brown and the toppings are bubbling. Check underneath with a metal spatula to ensure the bottom crust is deep brown too. Let the pizza rest for 5 minutes. Sprinkle with the cilantro, then cut the pizza into 8 wedges and serve.

CAROLINA PIE

Chicken ▲ Mandarin Oranges ▲ Roasted Red Peppers

**Corn Flour Pizza
Dough (page 140)**

**Roasted Red Pepper
Strips (page 32)**

**Roasted Chicken Breast
(page 35)**

**Herbed Olive Oil
(page 27)**

**1   ounce grated
Parmigiano
Reggiano (1/4 cup)**

**2 1/2 ounces fontina,
shredded (1 cup)**

**1   cup shredded
mozzarella**

**1   (15-ounce) can
mandarin orange
segments, drained**

**1   tablespoon chopped
fresh flat-leaf
parsley**

Raleigh is the capital of North Carolina, and
Capital Creations is the capital for pizza there.
This roasted chicken pizza captures the spirit of
Raleigh, a burgeoning cosmopolitan town full
of art, museums, sports, entertainment, and,
of course, pizza. The mellow fontina cheese,
brightened by mandarin orange segments and
roasted peppers, reminds me of how unexpectedly pleasant it is to be there.

MAKES 1 (12-INCH) PIZZA, SERVES 2

Make the pizza dough at least 12 hours ahead.
Rest the dough on the counter until it comes
to room temperature, about 1 hour. Make the
roasted red pepper strips, the roasted chicken
breast, and the herbed olive oil.

Move an oven rack to the lowest position.
Preheat the oven to 500°F for 30 minutes.

Shape the dough and place it on the pizza pan
or screen, according to the instructions on
page 141. Spread the herbed oil over the dough
with a pastry brush, covering the entire surface.
Sprinkle with the Parmigiano Reggiano. Toss the
shredded fontina and the mozzarella in a medium
bowl, and then sprinkle the cheeses over the
dough. Top with the orange segments and roasted
pepper strips. Thinly slice the roasted chicken
breast and arrange the pieces over the top.

Bake the pizza for about 15 minutes, until the
crust is deep brown and the toppings are bubbling. Check underneath with a metal spatula to
ensure the bottom crust is deep brown too. Let
the pizza rest for 5 minutes. Sprinkle with the
parsley, then cut the pizza into 8 wedges and
serve.

TRENTON TOMATO PIE WITH BABY CLAMS

Baby Clams ▲ Tomato Sauce ▲ Oregano

Corn Flour Pizza
  Dough (page 140)

Chunky Tomato Sauce
  (page 27)

1 tablespoon extra-
   virgin olive oil

1/2 cup minced onion

4 cloves garlic,
   minced

1 tablespoon dried
   oregano

1 (28-ounce) can baby
   clams, drained,
   or 36 fresh baby
   clams, shucked

Nonstick cooking spray

16 ounces fresh
   mozzarella, sliced
   into 1/2-inch-thick
   rounds

2 ounces grated
   Parmigiano
   Reggiano (1/2 cup)

**DELORENZO'S PIZZA,
HAMILTON, NEW JERSEY**

DeLorenzo's goes back to when Grandma and
Grandpa DeLorenzo lived in a small town in
Naples, Italy. Yes, it's another immigrant success story. We know how those go. Faced with
little or no opportunity, budding entrepreneurs
risk everything to come to America, where the
streets are paved in pizza sauce and dough rises
to the occasion. The DeLorenzos raised a family
of twelve kids from the proceeds of that first
pizza shop, which they opened in 1938. Let's lift
a glass to the DeLorenzos! *Cin cin!*

And here's to canned baby clams, too. You
may have to hunt them down, but it's worth it.
Plump baby clams are much more tender than
chopped clams, which come from big honkers
that are tough as rubber and cooked to death.
So find these babies, put them in your pie, and
discover the entrepreneurial magic that helped
create American pizza culture.

MAKES 1 (12-INCH) DEEP-DISH PIE, SERVES 4

Make the pizza dough at least 12 hours ahead.
Rest the dough on the counter until it comes to
room temperature, about 1 hour. Make the chunky
tomato sauce at least 1 hour before.

Move an oven rack to the lowest position.
Preheat the oven to 500°F for 30 minutes.

Heat the olive oil in a medium skillet over
medium-high heat. Sauté the onion, garlic, and
oregano for 1 minute, then add the baby clams
and toss to combine. Remove from the heat.

Spray a 12 x 2-inch deep-dish pizza pan with
nonstick cooking spray. Shape the dough for a
deep-dish pizza pan, according to the instructions

on page 141. Top with the mozzarella. Sprinkle
with 1/4 cup of the Parmigiano Reggiano. Pour the
clams over the cheese. Pour the tomato sauce
on top and sprinkle with the remaining 1/4 cup
Parmigiano Reggiano.

Bake the pizza for about 30 minutes, until the
crust is deep brown and the toppings are bubbling. Check underneath with a metal spatula to
ensure the bottom crust is deep brown too. Let
the pizza rest for 5 minutes. Cut it into 8 wedges
and serve.

NO. 6

Artichoke Hearts ▲ Goat Cheese ▲ Kalamata Olives

Corn Flour Pizza Dough (page 140)

Scant 1/2 cup blue cornmeal

1 cup peeled garlic cloves (about 40)

2 tablespoons olive oil

1/2 teaspoon salt

1/4 cup sun-dried tomatoes, sliced into strips

4 ounces baby spinach, packed, (about 4 cups)

1 ounce grated Parmigiano Reggiano (1/4 cup)

1 cup shredded mozzarella

1 (13.75-ounce) can artichoke hearts, drained and quartered

12 pitted kalamata olives, halved

4 ounces goat cheese

ROOFTOP PIZZERIA,
SANTA FE, NEW MEXICO

At Rooftop, you take the elevator up to the roof and dine outside while the sun sets over Santa Fe. You might be eating the blue corn crust, which lends sweetness and toasty corn taste to a goat cheese, olive, and baby spinach pie.

Rooftop Pizza might be the only place in America to serve a pie with a blue corn crust. Naturally, I wanted to re-create it. I found blue cornmeal, but it was a coarse grind, so I put it into my blender and gave it a spin for about thirty seconds. It poured out like blue corn dust, and I was ready to use it in my pizza dough.

I didn't want to peel an entire cup of garlic cloves for the roasted garlic paste, so I bought freshly peeled garlic cloves. I suggest you do the same. It seems like a lot of garlic on one pizza, but when you roast the cloves, the strong flavor mellows and sweetens.

MAKES 1 (12-INCH) PIZZA, SERVES 2 TO 3

Make the pizza dough at least 12 hours ahead, substituting blue corn flour for yellow: Pour the blue cornmeal into a blender and blend until fine, about 30 seconds. Measure the blue corn flour again to make sure it comes to 1/2 cup, before proceeding with the recipe. Rest the dough on the counter until it comes to room temperature, about 1 hour.

Preheat the oven to 500°F.

Place the garlic cloves in a small baking pan. Add 1 cup water, 1 tablespoon of the olive oil, and the salt. Roast for 1 hour, until the cloves are slightly browned, the liquid has reduced by half, and the garlic is soft. Mash the garlic and pan juices with

a rubber spatula to create a smooth paste. Keep the oven on.

While the garlic cooks, place the sun-dried tomatoes in a small bowl and cover with 1/2 cup hot water. Soak until soft, about 30 minutes. Squeeze out the excess water with your hands.

Heat the remaining 1 tablespoon olive oil in a medium skillet over medium-high heat. Sauté the spinach until limp, about 1 minute. When cool enough to handle, squeeze out the excess water.

Move an oven rack to the lowest position.

Shape the dough and place it on the pizza pan or screen, according to the instructions on

page 141. Spread the garlic paste over the dough with a rubber spatula, leaving a 1/2-inch border. Sprinkle with the Parmigiano Reggiano, followed by the mozzarella. Pat dry the artichoke hearts with paper towels before scattering the pieces on the pizza. Place little mounds of spinach, sun-dried tomato strips, and olives on top. Crumble the goat cheese over all.

Bake the pizza for about 20 minutes, until the crust is deep brown and the toppings are bubbling. Check underneath with a metal spatula to ensure the bottom crust is deep brown too. Let the pizza rest for 5 minutes. Cut it into 8 wedges and serve.

Why I Love Blue Corn

Developed by the Hopi Indians, blue corn has more protein than regular corn and a lower starch content. It's also higher in antioxidants and amino acids. But best of all, it's sweeter, nuttier, and toastier than regular corn.

For the Hopis, blue corn represents long life. Historically, they ate it when going on long journeys, formed into piki bread, a patty or flatbread. Now a staple of New Mexican cuisine, blue corn products—tortilla chips, enchiladas, and pancakes—are everywhere.

Some farmers' markets and co-ops sell locally produced grains milled for consumers. A fresher product means a boost in flavor and nutrients in flavor, and makes this artisan grain worth seeking out.

SALAD PIZZA

Roasted Red Peppers ▲ *Gorgonzola* ▲ *Salad*

Corn Flour Pizza
Dough (page 140)

$1/2$ teaspoon fennel
seeds

Roasted Red Pepper
Strips (page 32)

Sautéed Mushrooms
(page 34)

5 ounces fontina,
shredded (2 cups)

1 tablespoon extra-
virgin olive oil

1 tablespoon good-
quality balsamic
vinegar

$1/2$ teaspoon garlic
powder

2 ounces Gorgonzola,
crumbled ($1/2$ cup)

6 ounces spring salad
mix (about 6 cups)

Everyone's on a diet in California. They have beautiful weather year-round and want to keep fit to enjoy it. The rest of us throw on an over-size coat and order nachos. Even Californians need pizza, though. But how could they indulge and get that salad burn at the same time? Enter the Salad Pizza by Rustica. The Gorgonzola-dressed baby greens look majestically healthy atop a golden corn crust. A little fennel in the crust amplifies the corn flavor, and roasted peppers and mushrooms carry on the call for good health. This pizza works on many levels and it keeps Californians slim. Maybe it will work for the rest of us, too.

MAKES 1 (12-INCH) PIZZA, SERVES 2 TO 3

Make the pizza dough at least 12 hours ahead. Work the fennel seeds into the dough. Rest the dough on the counter until it comes to room temperature, about 1 hour. Make the roasted red pepper strips and the sautéed mushrooms.

Move an oven rack to the lowest position. Preheat the oven to 500°F for 30 minutes.

Shape the dough and place it on the pizza pan or screen, according to the instructions on page 141. Top with the shredded fontina, leaving a 1-inch border. Place the red peppers and mushrooms on top.

Bake the pizza for about 15 minutes, until the crust is deep brown and the toppings are bubbling. Check underneath with a metal spatula to ensure the bottom crust is deep brown too. Let the pizza rest for 5 minutes.

Mix the olive oil, vinegar, and garlic powder in a large bowl. Add the Gorgonzola and salad greens. Toss the greens with the cheese and the dressing to coat. Pile the tossed salad on the pizza, then cut it into 8 wedges and serve.

CORN PIZZA

Corn ▲ Smoked Cheese ▲ Balsamic Onion

Corn Flour Pizza Dough (page 140)

1 large red onion, peeled and thinly sliced

1 cup balsamic vinegar

12 ounces fresh mozzarella, cut into 1-inch cubes

1 tablespoon liquid smoke

1 cup fresh or frozen corn kernels

2 tablespoons butter, melted

1/4 cup chopped fresh chives

ZELO GOURMET CRUST PIZZA, ARCADIA, CALIFORNIA

At Zelo, the chefs must be purists, as all their pizzas have one-ingredient names. This must be how they communicate their passion to their guests. They know that when you see a pizza called Corn, the power to imagine a pizza filled with buttery corn will get people salivating. And that's what you get, along with a subtle smoked cheese and black onions roasted in balsamic vinegar.

MAKES 1 (12-INCH) PIZZA, SERVES 2

Make the pizza dough at least 12 hours ahead. Rest the dough on the counter until it comes to room temperature, about 1 hour. If using frozen corn, thaw and drain.

Preheat the oven to 400°F.

Spread the onion slices on a half sheet pan. Pour the balsamic vinegar over them and mix thoroughly with your hands or tongs. Roast for 20 minutes. The onion will become soft and will soak up most of the vinegar.

Move an oven rack to the lowest position. Increase the oven temperature to 500°F and heat for 15 minutes.

Put the mozzarella cubes in a reclosable bag with the liquid smoke. Shake the bag to coat all the pieces.

Shape the dough and place it on the pizza pan or screen, according to the instructions on page 141. Spread the marinated mozzarella chunks on top. Toss the corn kernels in a medium bowl with the melted butter. Pour the corn over the mozzarella and spread it out evenly. Place little mounds of the balsamic roasted onion on top.

Bake the pizza for about 20 minutes, until the crust is deep brown and the toppings are bubbling. Check underneath with a metal spatula to ensure the bottom crust is deep brown too. Let the pizza rest for 5 minutes. Sprinkle with the chives, then cut the pizza into 8 wedges and serve.

Chapter 9

WHOLE WHEAT PIZZAS

You might think these pizzas come from health food restaurants and are covered with sprouts. No way. These are fantastic pizzas from some of America's best restaurants.

These pizza places discovered that whole wheat could make a crust that's tender and nutty, and bakes to a crisp golden brown. So yes, this whole-grain pizza dough is more nutritious than regular dough and filled with antioxidants. But even more important is that it tastes good and handles like a dream.

All the recipes in this chapter are for 12-inch pizzas. There's a grilled pie from Al Forno, a fine dining restaurant in Rhode Island, the only grilled pizza in this book. You'll find everything from a traditional combination of fig jam and proscuitto to an outrageously great macaroni and cheese pizza that will rock your world.

WHOLE WHEAT PIZZA DOUGH

1/2 cup whole wheat flour

3/4 cup unbleached all-purpose flour, plus more for dusting

1/2 cup water

3 tablespoons plus 1 teaspoon extra-virgin olive oil

1 tablespoon white cornmeal

1 1/8 teaspoons active dry yeast

1/2 teaspoon sugar

1/2 teaspoon salt

Nonstick cooking spray

Some whole wheat pizzas are heavy, and maybe you've tried them without success. Now you can relax and enjoy this one. The ratio of whole wheat to regular flour is higher than most, yet this dough makes a crust so tender and light that you can substitute it for any of the pizzas in this cookbook. If you want more whole grains and fiber in your diet, this crust is a good way to feel better about eating your favorite food.

Whole wheat flour has a toasty, nutty flavor. It's brown because it contains the entire wheat germ. I recommend King Arthur or Bob's Red Mill brands. Usually blended with all-purpose flour, whole wheat is too heavy on its own and won't rise much, causing dense dough. I add white cornmeal, preferably Quaker brand, for crunch. You can also use cornmeal beneath a pizza on the peel for greater sliding capability.

Make this dough up to 3 days ahead. Let it come to room temperature for about 1 hour before using. Note that this crust takes less time to bake than some other crusts, about 12 minutes, so watch it carefully toward the end to make sure it doesn't burn.

MAKES ENOUGH DOUGH FOR 1 (12-INCH) PIZZA CRUST

Place the flours, water, 3 tablespoons of the olive oil, the cornmeal, yeast, and sugar in the bowl of a stand mixer fitted with the dough hook. Mix on low to combine, about 2 minutes.

Turn off the mixer and let the dough rest for about 10 minutes. Add the salt, then knead the

dough on medium speed for about 6 minutes, until the dough is firm, sticky, and supple. It will be soft, smooth, and shiny. If the dough seems too dry, add 1 or 2 teaspoons water.

Pour the remaining 1 teaspoon olive oil into a medium bowl. Shape the dough into a ball and place it in the bowl. Turn the dough to coat it with the oil. This prevents a crust from forming on its surface as it rises. Cover the bowl with plastic wrap and let the dough rise in the refrigerator for about 12 hours. It will double in volume. Rest the dough on the counter until it comes to room temperature, about 1 hour.

Get the Dough in Shape

STRETCH THE DOUGH Lightly flour a clean, dry countertop. Gently place the round of dough on your counter. Do not knead or press on it. Instead, let it settle. Dust the top with flour.

Make dimples in the dough with your fingertips by pressing down in the middle to stretch it out. Move the dough around in a circle as you continue to press down with your fingertips. A 1-inch rim should occur naturally. Press your fingertips along the inside of the rim, moving in a circle. Place your hands on the dough, fingers up against the rim, and push out while turning in a circle. Add more flour, if necessary, to ensure the dough slides easily.

Pick up the dough to finish stretching it out. Slide your hands underneath it and pick it up. Let the dough fall around your hands to stretch it. Keep your hands along the edges, rather than in the middle. The dough should be 12 inches in diameter, unless otherwise specified.

PLACE THE DOUGH ON THE PAN OR SCREEN Spray a 14-inch pizza pan with nonstick cooking spray and place it next to the shaped dough. Quickly pick up the shaped dough while sliding it onto the screen. Reshape as necessary. Your whole wheat dough is now ready for the pizza toppings.

SHANNON PIZZA

Prosciutto ▲ *Gorgonzola* ▲ *Figs*

Whole Wheat Pizza
Dough (page 158)

3 ounces dried figs,
chopped (about
$^1/_2$ cup)

$^1/_2$ cup apple juice

1 teaspoon butter

1 cup shredded
mozzarella

4 ounces thinly sliced
prosciutto

2 ounces Gorgonzola,
crumbled ($^1/_2$ cup)

2 scallions, chopped

Elizabeths is a fancy place with a woman's
touch. Both Elizabeths (there are two!) put their
blood and sweat into this stunning restaurant,
which looks like a mash-up of Queen Elizabeth
meets old Hollywood. It's far too glamorous for
a pizza restaurant, but I won't hold that against
the place.

Their pizzas have curious names like
Montgomery, Taylor, and Boop, harking back
to the days of high-society glamour. The fig and
Gorgonzola pie combines salty bites of proscu-
itto with rich Gorgonzola and sweet fig jam.
These ladies really know how to throw a party.

MAKES 1 (12-INCH) PIZZA, SERVES 2 TO 3

Make the pizza dough at least 12 hours ahead.
Rest the dough on the counter until it comes to
room temperature, about 1 hour.

Move an oven rack to the lowest position.
Preheat the oven to 500°F for 30 minutes.

Combine the figs, apple juice, and butter in a
small saucepan. Simmer over medium heat until
the figs are soft and all the liquid has evaporated,
about 10 minutes. Mash the figs with a fork until
they are a jammy consistency. If the figs are still
hard, return to the heat, add a few drops of water,
and cook for 1 or 2 minutes longer.

Shape the dough and place it on the pizza pan
or screen, according to the instructions on
page 159. Sprinkle with the mozzarella, leaving
a 1-inch border. Ball up the proscuitto slices and
tuck them around the pizza. Drop spoonfuls of
the fig jam on top.

Bake the pizza for about 13 minutes, until the
crust is deep brown and the toppings are bubbling. Check underneath with a metal spatula
to ensure the bottom crust is deep brown
too. Immediately sprinkle the pizza with the
Gorgonzola. Let the pizza rest for 5 minutes.
Sprinkle with the scallions, then cut the pizza into
8 wedges and serve.

THE LUAU

Ham ▲ Pineapple ▲ Spinach

Whole Wheat Pizza Dough (page 158)

Nonstick cooking spray

1 cup small fresh pineapple chunks

1 tablespoon extra-virgin olive oil

3 ounces packed baby spinach (about 3 cups), chopped

1 ounce grated Parmigiano Reggiano (1/4 cup)

1 cup shredded mozzarella

2 1/2 ounces fontina, shredded (1 cup)

12 ounces ham, finely chopped

The Luau pizza successfully conjures visions of Hawaii in this classic American combination. Pineapple pieces are caramelized to bring out their sweetness, which pairs nicely with salty ham. Wheat State Pizza, with branches in Manhattan, Topeka, and Lawrence, Kansas, makes gourmet pies emphasizing whole wheat crusts.

MAKES 1 (12-INCH) PIZZA, SERVES 2 TO 3

Make the pizza dough at least 12 hours ahead. Rest the dough on the counter until it comes to room temperature, about 1 hour.

Move an oven rack to the lowest position. Preheat the oven to 500°F for 30 minutes.

Spray a medium skillet with nonstick cooking spray and heat over high heat until smoking. Add the pineapple and spread it out in a single layer to sear, about 1 minute. The seared pineapple will have a caramelized side from contact with the pan. Transfer the pineapple to a colander set in the sink and drain.

Heat the olive oil in another medium skillet over medium heat. Quickly sauté the chopped spinach in the pan until it wilts, about 1 minute. Transfer to a colander set in the sink and drain.

Shape the dough and place it on the pizza pan or screen, according to the instructions on page 159. Sprinkle with the Parmigiano Reggiano, mozzarella, and fontina. Add small mounds of the cooked spinach. Top with the chopped ham and the seared pineapple chunks.

Bake the pizza for about 13 minutes, until the crust is deep brown and the toppings are bubbling. Check underneath with a metal spatula to ensure the bottom crust is deep brown too. Let the pizza rest for 5 minutes. Cut it into 8 wedges and serve.

PUNCTUATED EQUILIBRIUM PIZZA

Rosemary ▲ *Goat Cheese* ▲ *Kalamata Olives*

AMERICAN FLATBREAD,
BURLINGTON, VERMONT

Whole Wheat Pizza
Dough (page 158)

Roasted Red Pepper
Strips (page 32)

Herbed Olive Oil
(page 31)

All-purpose flour, for
dusting

Nonstick cooking spray

8   ounces goat
cheese, at room
temperature

1/4 cup grated Pecorino
Romano

12 pitted kalamata
olives, halved

1/2 red onion, peeled
and thinly sliced

1   tablespoon fresh
rosemary, chopped

Punctuated equilibrium is a theory proposing that most species will exhibit little evolutionary change for most of their history. This theory can be proved wrong simply by making flatbread. Once infected by the flatbread bug, you will sell all your belongings, quit your job, and become obsessed with flatbread pizza for seven years. That's what happened to me.

Typically flatbreads have fewer toppings than pizza. That is the main difference. This pretty pizza has a base of herbed goat cheese topped with roasted red peppers, purple kalamata olives, and red onion.

MAKES 1 (12-INCH) PIZZA, SERVES 2 TO 3

Make the pizza dough at least 12 hours ahead. Rest the dough on the counter until it comes to room temperature, about 1 hour. Make the red pepper strips and the herbed olive oil.

Move an oven rack to the lowest position. Preheat the oven to 500°F for 30 minutes.

Lightly flour a clean, dry countertop. Put the dough in the center and sprinkle a little flour on top. Roll out the dough using a rolling pin, starting from the center out to the edges. Work around the dough to form a circular crust with even thickness, about 12 inches in diameter. Pick up the shaped dough and fold it in half gently to transfer it to the pizza pan or screen sprayed with nonstick cooking spray. Unfold and flatten.

Slather the herbed oil onto the pizza with a pastry brush, covering the entire surface. Spread the goat cheese on the pizza in a thin layer using a rubber spatula. (If the cheese is not spreading well, pop the pizza in the oven for 30 seconds and it will melt.) Sprinkle with the Romano, peppers, onion, and rosemary.

Bake the pizza for about 13 minutes, until the crust is deep brown and the toppings are bubbling. Check underneath with a metal spatula to ensure the bottom crust is deep brown too. Let the pizza rest for 5 minutes. Cut it into 8 wedges and serve.

GRILLED PIZZA CALAMARI

Calamari ▲ *Spicy Tomato Sauce* ▲ *Lemon*

Whole Wheat Pizza Dough (page 158)

Chunky Tomato Sauce (page 27)

1   cup canola oil

1/2 cup flour, plus more for dusting

1/4 cup cornstarch

1/2 teaspoon sea salt

1/2 teaspoon cayenne pepper

1   pound cleaned squid and tentacles, bodies cut into rings

2   tablespoons extra-virgin olive oil

1   teaspoon Sriracha sauce

1/2 teaspoon crushed red pepper flakes

1   ounce grated Parmigiano Reggiano (1/4 cup)

1   cup shredded mozzarella

1   tablespoon chopped fresh flat-leaf parsley

1/2 lemon, thinly sliced

Two chefs, Johanne Killeen and her husband, George Germon, own Al Forno. These two have been cooking together for more than thirty-five years and are said to have been the first chefs to grill pizza.

This pizza is bursting with flavors and textures. There's the crispy char on the grilled pizza dough, a spicy tomato sauce, tender calamari, and refreshing bursts of lemon. Instead of an arrabiata sauce, I use my chunky tomato sauce, and amp up the pizza with a little Sriracha.

MAKES 1 (12-INCH) PIZZA, SERVES 2 TO 3

Make the pizza dough at least 12 hours ahead. Rest the dough on the counter until it comes to room temperature, about 1 hour. Make the chunky tomato sauce at least 1 hour ahead.

Preheat the oven to 200°F.

Heat the canola oil in a large pan over medium-high heat. Place the flour, cornstarch, salt, and cayenne in a large bowl. Add the squid pieces and toss in the flour to coat. (Test the oil temperature with one piece of squid. If it fries quickly, the oil is hot enough. If you have a deep-fry thermometer, the ideal temperature of the oil is 325°F.)

Fry the squid pieces in batches, to avoid over-crowding the pan. Cook until golden and crispy, about 3 minutes, turning once halfway through. Use a slotted spoon to transfer the squid to a baking sheet lined with paper towels. Remove the paper towels and keep the squid warm in the oven while you finish the pizza.

Heat an outdoor grill to medium-high. Hold your hand 6 inches from the surface and count to six. If your hand gets hot, the grill is ready.

Generously flour the back of a cookie sheet and lightly flour a clean, dry countertop. Put the dough in the center and sprinkle a little flour on top. Roll out the dough, using a rolling pin, starting

from the center out to the edges. Work around the dough to form a circular crust with even thickness, about 12 inches in diameter. Pick up the shaped dough, fold it in half, and gently transfer it to the back of the cookie sheet. Unfold and flatten.

Hold the cookie sheet close to the grill and slide the dough onto it. If the dough folds in on itself, move the edges out quickly to form a flat crust. Grill for about 3 minutes, without touching. Lift the underside of the crust with tongs to check it. It should be an even light brown with grill marks. Pick up the crust from the middle and transfer it back to the cookie sheet. Flip it over so the grilled side is facing up.

Mix the olive oil, Sriracha, and red pepper flakes in a small bowl. Brush half the spicy oil on the grilled side of the pizza crust and sprinkle with the Parmigiano Reggiano and mozzarella. Drop spoonfuls of the tomato sauce on top of the cheese. Do not spread out the sauce. Drizzle the remaining spicy oil over the pizza.

Slide the pizza onto the grill. Watch the pizza closely and turn the crust slightly during grilling to ensure it does not burn. The pizza will take 3 to 5 minutes to crisp and melt the cheese. Remove the pizza from the grill by sliding a pan beneath it and lifting it off the grill.

Place the warm calamari on the pizza. Sprinkle with the parsley and lemon slices, then cut the pizza into 12 wedges and serve.

CRAWFISH ÉTOUFFÉE PIZZA

Blackened Crawfish ▲ *Velveeta* ▲ *Salsa*

There's nothing like the sounds, tastes, bars, and bands of New Orleans. The next best thing to walking the streets and looking for a crawfish boil is to put on a Zydeco record, whip up some Hurricane cocktails, and enjoy this spicy crawfish étouffée pizza with friends.

Frozen crawfish tails are sold in one-pound bags, ready to thaw and prepare. Often you can find them at your local supermarket or seafood specialty store. You can make my blackening spice, aka Cajun Fairy Dust, or purchase it at most grocery stores. Commercial spice mixes are salty, so 2 tablespoons will do.

Whole Wheat Pizza Dough (page 158)

FOR THE BLACKENING SPICE BLEND

1½ tablespoons paprika

1 tablespoon garlic powder

1 tablespoon onion powder

1 tablespoon ground dried thyme

1 teaspoon kosher salt

1 teaspoon freshly ground black pepper

½ teaspoon cayenne pepper

1 teaspoon dried basil

1 teaspoon dried oregano

1 pound frozen cleaned cooked crawfish tails, thawed

2 tablespoons extra-virgin olive oil

8 ounces Velveeta

½ cup tomato salsa, preferably roasted

1 cup shredded mozzarella

1 cup shredded cheddar

½ cup chopped scallions

MAKES 1 (12-INCH) PIZZA, SERVES 2 TO 3

Make the pizza dough at least 12 hours ahead. Rest the dough on the counter until it comes to room temperature, about 1 hour.

Move an oven rack to the lowest position. Preheat the oven to 500°F for 30 minutes.

Make the Blackening Spice Blend: Combine all of the ingredients in a medium bowl and mix well.

Drain the crawfish by squeezing them to remove excess water. Add the crawfish to the bowl with the blackening spice and toss to coat.

Heat the olive oil in a medium skillet over high heat. Wait 3 minutes until the skillet is very hot before placing the crawfish in the pan in a single layer. You want each one to hit the hot pan. Do

not turn them over for about 3 minutes. Then stir and transfer to a bowl.

Put the Velveeta and salsa in a microwave-safe bowl and microwave on high for 1 minute. Stir, breaking up the cheese. Microwave for about 1 minute more. Stir the sauce until it is smooth and the cheese has completely melted.

Shape the dough and place it on the pizza pan or screen, according to the instructions on page 159. Toss the mozzarella and cheddar together in a medium bowl and sprinkle on the pizza, leaving a 1-inch border. Scatter the crawfish on top. Pour the cheese-salsa sauce over the toppings and spread it around with a rubber spatula.

Bake the pizza for about 13 minutes, until the crust is deep brown and the toppings are bubbling. Check underneath with a metal spatula to ensure the bottom crust is deep brown too. Let the pizza rest for 5 minutes. Sprinkle with the scallions, then cut the pizza into 8 wedges and serve.

BAKED MAC & CHEESE PIZZA

Macaroni ▲ *Four Cheeses* ▲ *Chives*

JIMMY THE GREEK'S, OLD ORCHARD BEACH, MAINE

Whole Wheat Pizza Dough (page 158)

FOR THE MAC AND CHEESE

Nonstick cooking spray

2   teaspoons salt

8   ounces small elbow macaroni

2   tablespoons butter

1/2 cup minced onion

2   tablespoons all purpose flour

1   teaspoon dry mustard

1/2 teaspoon paprika

1/4 teaspoon freshly ground black pepper

2   cups milk

16 ounces shredded sharp cheddar (4 cups)

1   cup shredded mozzarella

1   cup shredded cheddar

1/4 cup grated Pecorino Romano

12 crushed Ritz crackers (about 1/2 cup)

2   tablespoons chopped fresh chives

Mac and cheese on a pizza? Yes, please. Jimmy the Greek's pizza place serves this monolith of carbs every day. This pie may change your life—and your pant size, because you'll love the contrasting textures of creamy macaroni and crispy crust.

If you're wondering how to keep the mac and cheese on the pizza, I figured it out. I scrape it into a cake pan and refrigerate it. This creates a low-tech mac and cheese disc that holds its shape. You can make it up to three days in advance. Then you slide that sucker onto a whole wheat crust and bake it, for the best mac and cheese you will ever eat with your hands.

MAKES 1 (12-INCH) PIZZA, SERVES 4

Make the pizza dough at least 12 hours ahead. Rest the dough on the counter until it comes to room temperature, about 1 hour.

Make the Mac and Cheese: Spray a 10-inch round cake pan with nonstick cooking spray.

Boil 4 quarts water with 1 teaspoon of the salt. Add the macaroni and cook until al dente, 8 to 10 minutes. Drain the macaroni in a colander set in the sink, and transfer to a large bowl.

Melt the butter in a medium saucepan over medium heat. Add the onion and sauté for 30 seconds. Add the flour, remaining 1 teaspoon salt, the dry mustard, paprika, and pepper and stir continuously until a paste forms. Add the milk and stir continuously until smooth. Simmer for about 5 minutes, until thickened. Stir 1/4 cup of the sharp cheddar into the thickened sauce and keep stirring until it is smooth and melted.

Pour the cheese sauce over the macaroni and stir until it is all well combined. Scrape half of the mac and cheese into the prepared pan. Sprinkle with the remaining 1/4 cup cheddar. Pour the rest of the mac and cheese on top and pat it down to form a cake. Chill for 1 hour.

Move an oven rack to the lowest position. Preheat the oven to 500°F for 30 minutes.

Shape the dough and place it on the screen, according to the instructions on page 159. Sprinkle with the mozzarella, cheddar, and Romano. Use a metal spatula to loosen the mac

and cheese cake from the pan. Turn the pan over and carefully transfer the mac and cheese cake to a plate. Slide the mac and cheese onto the middle of the pizza, and top with the crushed crackers.

Bake the pizza for about 13 minutes, until the crust is deep brown and the mac and cheese is bubbling. Check underneath with a metal spatula to ensure the bottom crust is deep brown too. Let the pizza rest for 5 minutes. Sprinkle with the chives, then cut the pizza into 8 wedges and serve.

Chapter 10

GLUTEN-FREE PIZZAS

I've wanted to create a tasty gluten-free crust for years. This book gave me the opportunity. Now everyone, not just celiacs and the gluten-free crowd, can enjoy a great pizza crust whenever they want, simply because it tastes good.

Creating an excellent crust was a challenge. But after lots of reading and research, a conversation with Shauna Ahern of *Gluten-Free Girl and the Chef*, and several failed attempts, I've finally done it. It's thin and crispy on the outside, with a springy texture and good flavor. It took me dozens of tries to get it right, and I finally nailed it. Plus, once you get the ingredients, it comes together in a snap.

When you top this crust, you have lots of choices. All the recipes in this chapter come from restaurants that make a gluten-free pizza, so the toppings are gluten-free too. I use cornstarch in two recipes, as a thickener for sauces. Choose cornstarch made in a facility that avoids gluten cross-contamination, such as those from Argo and Kingsford's, Bob's Red Mill, and Clabber Girl.

GLUTEN-FREE PIZZA CRUST

1 cup potato starch

1 cup sweet rice flour

1 cup sorghum flour

1 tablespoon powdered unflavored psyllium

1 tablespoon dry powdered milk

1 tablespoon active dry yeast

1 tablespoon baking powder

1 teaspoon salt

1 teaspoon sugar

1 large egg, beaten

1/4 cup extra-virgin olive oil, plus 1 tablespoon for the bowl

2 cups warm water

Nonstick cooking spray

You might look at this recipe and wonder where you are going to get these strange ingredients. But it's not hard at all. I found them all either online or at a health food store.

Sorghum is the main flour, providing sweetness and structure to the dough. Ultra-fine potato starch makes crusts crisp and crunchy. Sweet rice flour adds flavor and lightness. Psyllium adds crunch and texture, and dry milk powder gives the crust flavor and richness.

This recipe makes two pizza doughs. You don't want to get all these ingredients for just one pizza! The batter is similar to pancake batter. After rising overnight in the refrigerator, you bake it like a thin cake layer, in a cake pan. Then you have a fantastic cooked crust that's ready to top and bake.

MAKES DOUGH FOR 2 (12-INCH) PIZZA CRUSTS

Place the potato starch, flours, psyllium, powdered milk, yeast, baking powder, salt, and sugar in the bowl of a stand mixer fitted with the paddle attachment. Mix on the lowest possible setting to avoid blowing fine flours everywhere. Then add the egg, 1/4 cup of the oil, and the warm water and mix on medium-low speed until smooth, about 2 minutes. The batter will be wet like cake or pancake batter.

Oil a bowl with 1 tablespoon of the olive oil and pour the batter into it. Cover with plastic wrap and chill overnight. The dough will not rise much but it will firm up and thicken and fill with bubbles.

Preheat the oven to 400°F.

Spray a 12-inch round cake or deep-dish pizza pan generously with nonstick cooking spray. Pour half the batter into the pan and spin it around to get the dough to spread out evenly.

Bake the crust for about 15 minutes, until firm. It will not be browned. Cool for 5 minutes before removing it from the pan. Spray a pizza screen or pan with nonstick cooking spray and place it over the top of the pan. Invert the pan and the crust should fall out onto the pan. If not, remove it with a spatula. The gluten-free crust is now ready for the pizza toppings. (Bake the second crust and use or freeze for up to 3 months.)

FINOCCHIO PIZZA

Fennel Marmalade ▲ Bacon ▲ Gouda

1 prebaked gluten-free crust (page 174)

FOR THE FENNEL MARMALADE

2 tablespoons extra-virgin olive oil

1/2 onion, peeled and thinly sliced

1 small bulb fennel, cored and thinly sliced (1 cup)

1 teaspoon salt

1/2 cup brown sugar

1/2 cup orange juice, plus more as needed

Zest and juice of 1 lime

8 ounces bacon (8 slices)

Nonstick cooking spray

2 1/4 ounces Gouda, shredded (1 cup)

1/4 cup chopped fennel fronds

Out in the Wild West, in the middle of Montana, there's a pizzeria named Biga Pizza. Chef Bob Marshall is the pizza chief round these parts. He uses local organic ingredients from the Great Plains and cooks from scratch. You'll love this sophisticated pizza with alternating bites of sweet and salty flavors, featuring jammy onion and fennel marmalade, bacon, and Gouda.

MAKES 1 (12-INCH) PIZZA, SERVES 2

Make and bake the gluten-free pizza crust beforehand, according to the instructions on page 174.

Make the Fennel Marmalade: Heat the olive oil in a saucepan over medium heat. Add the onion, fennel, and salt. Cover and cook, stirring occasionally, until the onion and fennel wilt and brown, about 10 minutes. Stir in the brown sugar and orange and lime juices, and reduce the heat to low. Simmer, uncovered and stirring occasionally, for about 45 minutes. Watch the sauce to make sure it doesn't burn. The marmalade is done when the sauce is bubbly, caramelized, and most of the liquid has evaporated. If the sauce dries while the fennel is still on the crunchy side, add a few drops of orange juice. Remove from the heat and stir in the lime zest.

Move an oven rack to the lowest position. Preheat the oven to 400°F for 30 minutes.

Place the bacon strips on a sheet pan and bake for 15 minutes. They will be partially cooked. Drain on paper towels. Let cool, then slice into 1-inch pieces.

Place the prebaked pizza crust on a pizza pan or screen sprayed with nonstick cooking spray. Sprinkle with the shredded Gouda. Drop spoonfuls of the fennel marmalade on top and scatter the bacon pieces over all.

Bake the pizza for about 30 minutes, until the crust is brown and the toppings are bubbling. Check underneath with a metal spatula to ensure the bottom crust is golden. Let the pizza rest for 5 minutes. Transfer to a cutting board, sprinkle with the chopped fennel fronds, cut into 8 wedges, and serve.

GREEN CHILE PORK PIZZA

Pork ▲ Green Chile ▲ Red Onion

1   prebaked gluten-free pizza crust (page 174)

1   pound ground pork

1   clove garlic, chopped

1   (8 ounce) can tomatillo (green) salsa

1   (4.5-ounce) can green chiles

1   tablespoon cornstarch

1   Roma tomato, chopped

Nonstick cooking spray

2   cups shredded mozzarella

1/4   cup thinly sliced red onion

1/4   cup chopped fresh cilantro (from about 1/4 bunch)

Beau Jo's is legendary among Colorado outdoor enthusiasts. Perhaps they like the company's dedication to the environment—particularly their use of solar and wind power to operate their stores. Or maybe it's Beau Jo's partnerships with other businesses to generate money for their community that endears them.

But most of all, Denver folks love Beau Jo's for its Rocky Mountain pies, especially the Green Chile Pork Pizza. My version starts with a quick pork chili that's loaded with flavor from green salsa and roasted green chiles. Then you top it with tomato, onion, and cilantro for additional bursts of flavor and color.

MAKES 1 (12-INCH) PIZZA, SERVES 2 TO 3

Make and bake the gluten-free pizza crust beforehand, according to the instructions on page 174.

Move an oven rack to the lowest position. Preheat the oven to 400°F for 30 minutes.

Brown the pork over medium-high heat in a medium skillet, about 5 minutes. Add the chopped garlic, salsa, half the can of green chiles, 2 tablespoons water, and the cornstarch. Reduce the heat to low and cook for about 10 minutes, until the sauce is thick.

Mix the chopped tomatoes and the remaining green chiles together in a small bowl.

Place the prebaked pizza crust on a pizza pan or screen sprayed with nonstick cooking spray. Sprinkle with the mozzarella. Spread the green chile pork all the way out to the edges with a rubber spatula. Top with the tomato–green chile and the raw onion.

Bake the pizza for about 30 minutes, until the crust is brown and the toppings are bubbling. Check underneath with a metal spatula to ensure the bottom crust is golden. Let the pizza rest for 5 minutes. Transfer to a cutting board, sprinkle with the chopped cilantro, cut into 8 wedges, and serve.

GRILLED PEAR PIZZA

Pear ▲ *Bacon* ▲ *Gruyère*

1   prebaked gluten-free pizza crust (page 174)

1   clove garlic, chopped

1   tablespoon extra-virgin olive oil

8   ounces bacon (8 strips)

2   ripe pears, cored and thinly sliced

Nonstick cooking spray

6   ounces Gruyère, shredded (2 cups)

2   tablespoons chopped fresh flat-leaf parsley

In a historic town in the New Hampshire countryside, Red Fox makes wood-fired pizza from a stone oven. You can make the restaurant's Grilled Pear Pizza by grilling the pear slices in bacon fat to soften and char them. Then arrange them with the bacon and Gruyère for an irresistibly silky, salty, and sweet pizza.

MAKES 1 (12-INCH) PIZZA, SERVES 2 TO 3

Make and bake the gluten-free pizza crust beforehand, according to the instructions on page 174.

Move an oven rack to the lowest position. Preheat the oven to 400°F for 30 minutes.

Mix the garlic and the olive oil in a small bowl.

Place the bacon strips on a sheet pan and bake for 15 minutes. They will be partially cooked. Drain on paper towels. Let cool, then slice into 1-inch pieces. Put 2 tablespoons of the bacon fat into a large bowl. Add the pears and toss to coat.

Heat a medium skillet over medium-high heat. Place the pear slices in a single layer on the hot surface. You may need to work in batches. Cook each side for about 2 minutes, until charred and slightly soft. Turn the slices with a fork to avoid breaking them. Transfer the charred pears to a plate.

Place the prebaked pizza crust on a pizza pan or screen sprayed with nonstick cooking spray. Spread the garlic oil over the crust with a pastry brush, all the way out to the edges. Sprinkle with the Gruyère and distribute the pear slices on top in overlapping circles. Scatter the bacon pieces over all.

Bake the pizza for about 30 minutes, until the crust is brown and the toppings are bubbling. Check underneath with a metal spatula to ensure the bottom crust is golden too. Let the pizza rest for 5 minutes. Transfer to a cutting board, sprinkle with the parsley, cut into 8 wedges, and serve.

HAM N' CHEDDAR

Cheddar Spread ▲ Ham ▲ Chives

1   prebaked gluten-free crust (page 174)

Nonstick cooking spray

8   ounces sharp cheddar cheese spread, such as Merkts, at room temperature

1/2 pound thinly sliced ham, cut into ribbons

1   cup shredded sharp cheddar

2   tablespoons chopped fresh chives

This pizzeria claims to have the coldest beer in Arkansas. What a claim to fame! But cold beer is the perfect accompaniment to this super-simple, salty pizza that comes together in a snap. Cheddar and ham are a time-honored combination for a good reason. As soon as you find a sharp cheddar spread, you're in business.

MAKES 1 (12-INCH) PIZZA, SERVES 2 TO 3

Make and bake the gluten-free pizza crust beforehand, according to the instructions on page 174.

Move an oven rack to the lowest position. Preheat the oven to 400°F for 30 minutes.

Place the prebaked pizza crust on a pizza pan sprayed with nonstick cooking spray. Spread the cheddar cheese spread on the crust with a rubber spatula, all the way out to the edges. Cover with the ham, followed by the shredded cheddar cheese.

Bake the pizza for about 30 minutes, until the crust is brown and the toppings are bubbling. Check underneath with a metal spatula to ensure the bottom crust is golden too. Let the pizza rest for 5 minutes. Transfer to a cutting board, sprinkle with the chives, cut into 8 wedges, and serve.

CHICKEN CURRY AND YAM PIZZA

Chicken ▲ *Sweet Potato* ▲ *Mango Chutney*

ZPIZZA,
HONOLULU, HAWAII

1 prebaked gluten-free pizza crust (page 174)

1 small sweet potato

Roasted Chicken Breast (page 35)

FOR THE CURRY GLAZE

1/4 cup honey

2 teaspoons curry powder

1/4 teaspoon crushed red pepper flakes

FOR THE MANGO CHUTNEY

1 large mango, pitted, peeled, and diced

1/4 cup raisins

1 teaspoon grated fresh ginger

1 cup pineapple juice

1 teaspoon cornstarch

2 tablespoons sugar

2 tablespoons apple cider vinegar

Nonstick cooking spray

1 cup shredded mozzarella

2 tablespoons chopped fresh cilantro

The ZPizza chain of restaurants began in Laguna Beach, California. It is a leader in creating healthful gourmet pizzas, offering not only vegan but also many gluten-free pizzas adapted from its original menu. This is a somewhat sweet pizza that gets a kick from curry and chutney. If you adore sweet potatoes, this pizza has your name on it.

MAKES 1 (12-INCH) GLUTEN-FREE PIZZA, SERVES 2 TO 3

Make and bake the pizza crust beforehand, according to the instructions on page 174.

Move an oven rack to the lowest position. Preheat the oven to 400°F for 30 minutes.

Place the sweet potato on a sheet pan and roast for about 45 minutes, until very soft. (Roast the chicken on the pan at the same time.) Let cool; peel and slice into 12 chunks.

Make the Curry Glaze: Place all the ingredients in a small bowl and stir until combined.

Make the Mango Chutney: Put all the ingredients in a small saucepan and bring to a boil over medium-high heat. Reduce the heat to low and simmer, stirring occasionally, until the sauce thickens and reduces by half, about 10 minutes.

Place the prebaked pizza crust on a pizza pan sprayed with nonstick cooking spray. Sprinkle with the mozzarella. Slice the chicken and scatter it over the top. Add the mango chutney by teaspoons, followed by the pieces of sweet potato. Drizzle the top with the curry glaze.

Bake the pizza for about 30 minutes, until the crust is brown and the toppings are bubbling. Check underneath with a metal spatula to ensure the bottom crust is golden too. Let the pizza rest for 5 minutes. Transfer to a cutting board, sprinkle with the cilantro, cut into 8 wedges, and serve.

PIZZA VERA CRUZ

Honey-Chipotle Chicken ▲ Smoked Cheddar ▲ Red Pepper

1   prebaked gluten-
    free pizza crust
    (page 174)

**Roasted Chicken Breast
(page 35)**

**FOR THE HONEY-
CHIPOTLE SAUCE**

1   (8-ounce) can
    tomato puree or
    sauce

1   or 2 chipotle
    peppers in adobo
    sauce, minced

1/4 cup honey

1/2 teaspoon salt

1   tablespoon chopped
    fresh cilantro

Nonstick cooking spray

5   ounces smoked
    cheddar, shredded
    (2 cups)

1/2 red bell pepper, cut
    into thin strips

1/4 cup thinly sliced
    garlic cloves

1/2 cup chopped
    scallions

Taos calls people to spiritual awareness, to commune with incomparable beauty and serenity. The town is unconventional, relaxed, and informal. Taos Outback fits right in. To get there, you take a gravel driveway to a house turned restaurant. Tables and chairs are strewn throughout the yard as if a party has just disbanded. Several 1940s-style gasoline pumps provide more atmosphere.

The Pizza Vera Cruz is a little like a barbecued chicken pizza, but with lots more character. Smoked cheddar adds a hint of fire, and a honey-chipotle sauce kicks the flavor out into the stratosphere.

MAKES 1 (12-INCH) GLUTEN-FREE PIZZA, SERVES 2 TO 3

Make and bake the gluten-free pizza crust beforehand, according to the instructions on page 174. Make the roasted chicken breast.

Make the Honey-Chipotle Sauce: Put the tomato puree, chipotle peppers, honey, and salt in a small saucepan over medium heat. Reduce the heat to low and simmer, stirring occasionally, for about 15 minutes. Remove from the heat and stir in the cilantro.

Move an oven rack to the lowest position. Preheat the oven to 400°F for 30 minutes.

Place the prebaked pizza crust on a pizza pan or screen sprayed with nonstick cooking spray. Spread the sauce on the crust with a rubber

spatula, all the way out to the edges. Sprinkle with the smoked cheddar. Slice the chicken and scatter the pieces over the top, followed by the bell pepper and garlic.

Bake the pizza for about 30 minutes, until the crust is brown and the toppings are bubbling. Check underneath with a metal spatula to ensure the bottom crust is golden too. Let the pizza rest for 5 minutes. Transfer to a cutting board, sprinkle with the scallions, cut into 8 wedges, and serve.

Conversion Chart

All conversions are approximate.

LIQUID CONVERSIONS		WEIGHT CONVERSIONS		OVEN TEMPERATURES		
U.S.	Metric	U.S./U.K.	Metric	°F	Gas Mark	°C
1 tsp	5 ml	$1/2$ oz	14 g	250	$1/2$	120
1 tbs	15 ml	1 oz	28 g	275	1	140
2 tbs	30 ml	$1^{1}/2$ oz	43 g	300	2	150
3 tbs	45 ml	2 oz	57 g	325	3	165
$1/4$ cup	60 ml	$2^{1}/2$ oz	71 g	350	4	180
$1/3$ cup	75 ml	3 oz	85 g	375	5	190
$1/3$ cup + 1 tbs	90 ml	$3^{1}/2$ oz	100 g	400	6	200
$1/3$ cup + 2 tbs	100 ml	4 oz	113 g	425	7	220
$1/2$ cup	120 ml	5 oz	142 g	450	8	230
$2/3$ cup	150 ml	6 oz	170 g	475	9	240
$3/4$ cup	180 ml	7 oz	200 g	500	10	260
$3/4$ cup + 2 tbs	200 ml	8 oz	227 g	550	Broil	290
1 cup	240 ml	9 oz	255 g			
1 cup + 2 tbs	275 ml	10 oz	284 g			
$1^{1}/4$ cups	300 ml	11 oz	312 g			
$1^{1}/3$ cups	325 ml	12 oz	340 g			
$1^{1}/2$ cups	350 ml	13 oz	368 g			
$1^{2}/3$ cups	375 ml	14 oz	400 g			
$1^{3}/4$ cups	400 ml	15 oz	425 g			
$1^{3}/4$ cups + 2 tbs	450 ml	1 lb	454 g			
2 cups (1 pint)	475 ml					
$2^{1}/2$ cups	600 ml					
3 cups	720 ml					
4 cups (1 quart)	945 ml (1,000 ml is 1 liter)					

Pizzeria Guide

ALABAMA

Trattoria Centrale
207A 20th Street North
Birmingham, AL
(205) 202-5612
www.trattoriacentrale.com

ARIZONA

Damgoode Pies
3604 Walnut Street
Rogers, AZ
(479) 636-7437
plus other locations in AZ
www.damgoodepies.com

Pizzeria Bianco
multiple locations in Phoenix, AZ
www.pizzeriabianco.com

The Parlor Pizzeria
1916 E. Camelback Road
Phoenix, AZ
(602) 248-2480
www.theparlor.us

ARKANSAS

U.S. Pizza Company
multiple locations in AR
www.uspizzaco.net

CALIFORNIA

Caioti Pizza Café
4346 Tujunga Avenue
Studio City, CA
(818) 761-3588
www.caiotipizzacafe.com

Flour + Water
2401 Harrison Street
San Francisco, CA
(415) 826-7000
www.flourandwater.com

Pizza Orgasmica
multiple locations in
San Francisco, CA
www.pizzaorgasmica.com

Pizza Rustica Cafe
5422 College Avenue
Oakland, CA
(510) 654-1601
www.caferustica.com

Pizzeria Delfina
multiple locations in
San Francisco, CA
www.pizzeriadelfina.com

Pizzeria Mozza
641 N. Highland Avenue
Los Angeles, CA
(323) 297-0101
plus other locations in CA
www.pizzeriamozza.com

Zelo Gourmet Crust Pizza
328 E. Foothill Boulevard
Arcadia, CA
(626) 358-8298
www.myzelopizza.info

COLORADO

Beau Jo's
2710 S. Colorado Boulevard
Denver, CO
(303) 758-1519
plus other locations in CO
www.beaujos.com

CONNECTICUT

Frank Pepe Pizzeria Napoletana
163 Wooster Street
New Haven, CT
(203) 865-5762
plus other locations in CT and NY
www.pepespizzeria.com

DELAWARE

Nicola Pizza
8 N. 1st Street
Rehoboth, DE
(302) 227-6211
plus another location in DE
www.nicolapizza.com

Pizza by Elizabeths
3801 Kennett Pike
Greenville, DE
(302) 654-4478
www.pizzabyelizabeths.com

FLORIDA

Fratelli la Bufala
437 Washington Avenue
Miami Beach, FL
(305) 532-0700
www.flbmiami.com

GEORGIA

Varasano's Pizzeria
2171 Peachtree Road NE
Atlanta, GA
(404) 352-8216
www.varasanos.com

HAWAII

ZPizza
1200 Ala Moana Boulevard
Honolulu, HI
(808) 596-0066
plus many locations nationwide
www.zpizza.com

IDAHO

Flying Pie Pizza
multiple locations in Boise, ID,
and Meridian, ID
www.flyingpie.com

ILLINOIS

Gino's East
multiple locations in Chicago, IL
www.ginoseast.com

Uno Pizzeria & Grill
multiple locations nationwide
www.unos.com

IOWA

**McCaffrey's Dolcé Vita &
Twin Springs Bakery**
2149 Twin Springs Road
Decorah, IA
(563) 382-4723
www.mcdolcevita.com

KANSAS

Lomato's Pizza
130 W. 9th Street
Hays, KS
(785) 623-2888
www.lomatoshays.com

Wheat State Pizza
The Malls Shopping Center,
711 W. 23rd Street
Lawrence, KS
plus another location in KS
(785) 865-2323
www.wheatstatepizza.com

KENTUCKY

Impellizzeri's Pizza
multiple locations in Louisville, KY
www.impellizzeris.com

LOUISIANA

Louisiana Pizza Kitchen
615 S. Carrollton Avenue
New Orleans, LA
(504) 866-5900
www.louisianapizzakitchenuptown
.com

MAINE

Jimmy the Greek's
215 Saco Avenue
Old Orchard Beach, ME
(207) 934-7499
www.jimmygreeksopa.com

Pizza Napoli
667 Main Street
Ogunquit, ME
(207) 646-0303
www.pizzanapoliogunquit.com

MARYLAND

Joe Squared
133 W. North Avenue
Baltimore, MD
(410) 545-0444
plus another location in MD
www.joesquared.com

MASSACHUSETTS

Santarpio's
111 Chelsea Street
East Boston, MA
(617) 567-9871
plus another location in MA
www.santarpiospizza.com

MICHIGAN

**Buddy's Restaurant
and Pizzeria**
17125 Conant Street
Detroit, MI
(313) 892-9001
plus other locations in MI
www.buddyspizza.com

Motor City Brewing Works
470 W. Canfield Street
Detroit, MI
(313) 832-2700
www.motorcitybeer.com

MINNESOTA

Sven & Ole's
9 W. Wisconsin Street
Grand Marais, MN
(218) 387-1713
www.svenandoles.com

MISSISSIPPI

Old Venice Pizza Co.
1112 Van Buren Avenue
Oxford, MS
(662) 236-6872
plus other locations in MS and TN
www.oldvenice.com

MISSOURI

Imo's Pizza
multiple locations in MO
www.imospizza.com

MONTANA

Biga Pizza
241 W. Main Street
Missoula, MT
(406) 728-2579
www.bigapizza.com

NEBRASKA

**Big Fred's Restaurant
and Lounge**
1101 S. 119th Street
Omaha, NE
(402) 333-4419
www.bigfredsinc.com

NEVADA

Metro Pizza
multiple locations in NV
www.metropizza.com

NEW HAMPSHIRE

Red Fox Bar & Grille
49 US Route 16
Jackson, NH
(603) 383-4949
www.redfoxbarandgrille.com

NEW JERSEY

DeLorenzo's Pizza
147 Sloan Avenue
Hamilton, NJ
(609) 393-2952
www.delorenzospizza.com

NEW MEXICO

Rooftop Pizzeria
60 E. San Francisco Street
Santa Fe, NM
(505) 984-0008
www.rooftoppizzeria.com

Taos Pizza Outback
712 Paseo Del Pueblo Norte
Taos, NM
(575) 758-3112
www.taospizzaoutback.com

NEW YORK

Famous Ben's Pizza
multiple locations in New York, NY
www.famousbenspizzaofsoho.com

Pappardelle's Pizzeria
544 Stewart Avenue
Bethpage, NY
(516) 433-2463
www.pappardelles-hub.com

Patsy's Pizzeria
multiple locations in New York, NY
www.patsyspizzerianewyork.com

Roberta's Pizza
261 Moore Street
Brooklyn, NY
(718) 417-1118
www.robertaspizza.com

**Umberto's Pizzeria
& Restaurant**
633 Jericho Turnpike
New Hyde Park, NY
(516) 437-7698
www.originalumbertos.com

NORTH CAROLINA

Asheville Brewing Company
675 Merrimon Avenue
Asheville, NC
(828) 254-1281
www.ashevillebrewing.com

**Capital Creations
Gourmet Pizza**
1842 Wake Forest Road
Raleigh, NC
(919) 836-8000
www.capitalcreations.com

OHIO

Pizza Tower
8945 Governors Way
Cincinnati, OH
(513) 683-8400
www.pizzatower.com

OREGON

Apizza Scholls
4741 SE Hawthorne Boulevard
Portland, OR
(503) 233-1286
www.apizzascholls.com

Dove Vivi
2727 NE Glisan Street
Portland, OR
(503) 239-4444
www.dovevivipizza.com

PENNSYLVANIA

Jigsy's Old Forge Pizza
225 N. Enola Road
Enola, PA
(717) 732-7700
www.jigsyspizza.com

Osteria
640 N. Broad Street
Philadelphia, PA
(215) 763-0920
plus one NJ location
www.osteriaphilly.com

**Romano's Pizzeria and
Italian Restaurant**
246 Wanamaker Avenue
Essington, PA
(610) 521-9010
www.romanostromboli.com

RHODE ISLAND

Al Forno
577 S. Water Street
Providence, RI
(401) 273-9760
www.alforno.com

SOUTH CAROLINA

Humble Crumb
2521 Highmarket Street
Georgetown, SC
(843) 546-7090
www.thehumblecrumb.com

SOUTH DAKOTA

Big Time Pizza
At The Roosevelt Inn
206 Old Cemetery Road
Keystone, SD
(605) 666-4443
www.rosyinn.com

TEXAS

Dolce Vita Pizzeria Enoteca
500 Westheimer Road
Houston, TX
(713) 520-8222
www.dolcevitahouston.com

UTAH

Pizzeria Seven Twelve
320 S. State Street #185
Orem, UT
(801) 623-6712
www.pizzeria712.com

VERMONT

American Flatbread
115 Saint Paul Street
Burlington, VT
(802) 861-2999
plus more locations in VT
www.americanflatbread.com

WASHINGTON

Serious Pie
multiple locations in Seattle, WA
www.seriouspieseattle.com

WISCONSIN

Streetza Pizza
2201 S. 84th Street
Milwaukee, WI
(414) 215-0021
www.streetza.com

WYOMING

Pizza Place
218 S. Main Street
Lusk, WY
(307) 334-3000
www.facebook.com/pages/
The-Pizza-Place

Index